Other Books in the Historic Restaurants Series™

Florida's Historic Restaurants and Their Recipes
by Dawn O'Brien and Becky Roper Matkov

Georgia's Historic Restaurants and Their Recipes
by Dawn O'Brien and Jean Spaugh

Alabama's Historic Restaurants and Their Recipes
by Gay Martin

North Carolina's Historic Restaurants and Their Recipes

North Carolina's Historic Restaurants and Their Recipes

By Dawn O'Brien

John F. Blair, Publisher
Winston-Salem, North Carolina

Fourth Revised Edition

First Printing, 2004

DESIGN BY DEBRA LONG HAMPTON

MAP BY LASSITER & CO.

INTERIOR PHOTOGRAPHS BY DAWN O'BRIEN OR COURTESY OF THE RESTAURANT

PHOTOGRAPH ON FRONT COVER BY LESTER DUSTIN PECK

PHOTOGRAPH ON BACK COVER COURTESY OF THE CAROLINA INN

Library of Congress Cataloging-in-Publication Data

O'Brien, Dawn.

North Carolina's historic restaurants and their recipes / by Dawn O'Brien.-- 4th ed.

p. cm.

Includes index.

ISBN 0-89587-300-1 (alk. paper)

1. Cookery--North Carolina. 2. Restaurants--North Carolina.

3. Historic buildings--North Carolina. I. Title.

TX715.O285 2004

641.59756--dc22

2004008561

Preface

oday I sit at a laptop instead of the trusty old typewriter that was used to type my first historic restaurant book. That Smith Corona never required an electrical outlet, nor did it swallow entire articles whole, with no chance of retrieval, like my bug-prone computer has. Sometimes older things are better than new.

Maybe that's why I love well-crafted historic buildings. I am particularly drawn to historic buildings that have been recycled into great restaurants. In fact, when I asked owner/chef Mary Bacon why she chose a historic restaurant for her cosmopolitan restaurant, she said: "I love old buildings. It's as an artist once said: 'The beautiful young (people) are acts of nature; the beautiful old (people or buildings) are acts of art.' Those buildings have quality and memories that the new don't have."

Right. I feel the same way. I love old buildings because of the integrity of their craftsmanship and for the stories that preserve their pasts. Some of the buildings that are now restaurants were former textile mills, like Pewter Rose Bistro; some were elegant homes of famous politicians, like Gabrielle's at the Richmond Hill Inn, Second Empire, and The McNinch House. Others were grand inns, like Asheville's Grove Park, or Pinehurst's Holly Inn, which catered to the middle-class. Even with their aging aches and pains, these charming structures still surpass most new construction. In my opinion, much new construction lacks architectural beauty. Today's building materials don't seem ready to endure for the ages, and there is no evidence of the dedication and talent that those long-gone craftsmen brought to their work.

But guess what? Today I am seeing a resurgence of that work ethic in what restaurant customers now call "Star Chefs." This new breed of chefs is talented, modest, and sharing—hot items indeed. With their energy and creativity, they pay tribute to the previous generation of master chefs who taught them well.

Many of this new generation of chefs, male and female, may not have graduated from a revered cooking school. They learned from master chefs of America, Europe, and Asia, working as apprentices and soaking up the equivalent of advanced degrees in kitchen knowledge.

Fifty years ago in Europe, boys of fourteen were apprenticed to master chefs. After a lengthy apprenticeship, the young chefs continued their education by working for other famous chefs. Today, experienced younger chefs sometimes pay for the privilege of apprenticing with a grand master. Each step brings them closer to achieving their personal goals for food of the highest quality. Everyone benefits from this sort of dedication. Who doesn't love going to a restaurant where the chef is "all about" food?

Chefs of this sort—and we have plenty in North Carolina—spend their lives creating and adapting recipes. They've learned to imagine a taste and then set out to recreate it. I'll bet they dream recipes.

"Cooking is science and art," said chef Bill Stein of River House. "That is what gives us the ability to control and manipulate flavor." Stein began his career by apprenticing with Gayle Winston, the famous chef who now owns River House Restaurant. After a few years Stein left Winston to study in France with other great chefs. He learned different techniques from every chef with whom he worked, he said. Each master chef shaped and opened his mind in a new way.

Perhaps the most important thing he learned was to use fresh foods from the region in which you cook and create. Our state's many diverse regions produce truckloads of excellent ingredients and have access to fresh fish, fowl, pork, and beef. They speak with one voice on this: "Cook with what is organically grown from trusted locals." Our creative Tar Heel chefs love this access, but they also don't hesitate to order top-quality ingredients from wherever necessary to create their fare. The Internet has been a boon for these chefs as they seek out the exotic oils, chocolates, truffles, and freshest lamb, beef, and fish. One restaurateur has Norwegian salmon flown in twice a week, but she only uses that salmon on the day it arrives. Several insist that their breads be cooked in brick ovens. This is *la difference* that makes each chef unique.

How the restaurants were chosen

In 2003 the president of John F. Blair Publisher, Carolyn Sakowski, decided that a total rewrite of my first guidebook/cookbook was in order. I was thrilled to have the opportunity. When the Blair staff and I set about to do the rewrite, no one knew how many of the book's original restaurants remained. What really shocked us was the number of historic restaurants that needed to be added. More than two-thirds are new additions. Naturally each restaurant would have to meet the main requirement and be in a building at least fifty years old. Some of the restaurants are in buildings distinguished enough to be on the National Register of Historic Places. Of course, the quality of the food is equally important.

This is the first time that I have included chefs' names. In earlier editions, I didn't name them because many chefs change jobs frequently to study with other chefs and advance their careers. I didn't want my readers to go to a restaurant expecting the chef they had read about and be disappointed to find that he or she had moved on. But in 2004, there is great stability to be found throughout North Carolina's historic restaurants. Most of the chefs that I have named either own the restaurant or have been with the restaurant for over ten years.

Acknowledgments

I t takes the help of a whole state of angels in order for me to write a historic restaurant book. Since this is a guidebook/ cookbook, it entails a lot of travel, writing, cooking, and assemblage of history to make it come together. The angels who helped me with part or all of those needs are cherished gifts, especially when you find yourself wandering around in the dark trying to find your hotel or the bed-and-breakfast that your local angel has booked for you.

The most difficult thing about writing these books is trying to get busy chefs, who have very long hours, to send you their recipes. In desperation you call the local angel near the restaurant to see if he or she can persuade the chef to follow through. Though that is not part of his or her job, the angels delivered.

Those recipe-begging angels include Kory Patterson with the Convention & Visitors Bureau of Pinehurst and Janeen Driscoll, who is the Communication Manager for Pinehurst; another is Connie Nelson with Cape Fear Coast Convention & Visitors Bureau, who steered me away from a hurricane's path. Debbie Vargas of Greenville-Pitt County Convention & Visitors Bureau put me on to a fantastic restaurant that I would not have known about. Gail Murphy of the Greensboro Area Convention & Visitors Bureau has gone way out of her way to help so many times that she's probably wearing a halo.

Hendersonville Travel and Tourism for years has put me on to the right historic restaurants and paved rocky paths for me. I especially want to thank Melody Heltman and Karen Baker who went after my needs like "a dog with a bone." "No" is not in their vocabulary.

New Bern's Craven County Convention & Visitors Center was particularly efficient, especially Tarshi McCoy, who anticipated my next problem and was working on it before I was even aware of the problem. And one male angel, Martin Armes, of the Greater Raleigh Convention and Visitors Bureau, continually checked on me to see if all was running smoothly. Quinn Capps of Manteo and the Barrier Islands Convention & Visitors Bureau has even helped me out with other convention bureaus. The same kudos apply for the chambers of commerce in Ocracoke and Beaufort's Carol Lohr, who is with The Crystal Coast's Tourism Authority.

One reason that I've written so much about Winston-Salem is because of the help I received from their Convention & Visitors Bureau, especially Lynn Fuhler and Courtney Hobbs. Last—but definitely not least—is the photographer, writer, and innkeeper of Oscar's House on Ocracoke, Ann Ehringhaus. When I couldn't get to Ocracoke to take a photograph because hurricane-ravaged roads were impassable, divine intervention in the form of Ehringhaus stepped forward. She solved my problem by mailing me the photo, pronto. There is a special niche in heaven for this angel.

Contents

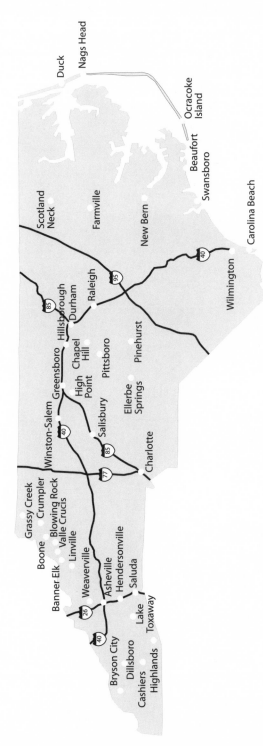

North Carolina

The Lifesaving Station
Restaurant at The Sanderling

N.C. 12

DUCK

$\mathcal{I}$n 1874, W. G. Partridge became the first keeper of U.S. Life Saving Station No. 5 at Caffey's Inlet. He was paid a whopping two hundred dollars a year. Each of the station's six original surfmen was given a small living area with a tiny closet. One such area has been retained to show the modest life of those courageous men.

Both wages and times have changed on the narrow strip of the Outer Banks where No. 5 still sits. Rebuilt in 1899, it was converted into an up-market nature restaurant with an adjacent inn in 1982.

On my second visit to The Sanderling, I was accompanied by my friend Jane Brock. We watched a Key West-type sunset color the sky to a vivid red coral as we were checking in. Sure, the sun sets everywhere, but it lacks the clarity you find here.

The redecorated dining room still wears its classic simplicity but now has a tonier feel. The cuisine is French-inspired. Our appetizer was Tomato and Herb Soup. When you use fresh—not canned or frozen—ingredients, any food will taste better. The right amount of seasoning, the fresh herbs, and the vine-grown tomatoes gave this soup a tangy taste that still fell within the comfort-food range. Plus, the bread—paired to each course here—proved a wholesome, perfect complement to the soup. It's the little things that distinguish salads from "same-olds." The Lifesaving Station's secret is three ingredients: raisins soaked in sherry, walnuts, and the combination of sherry vinegar and walnut oil. Jane shared her Flounder Stuffed with Jumbo Lump Crabmeat, served over Braised Belgian Endive with Caper Butter Sauce. It had a luxuriously tender but meaty taste. I ordered the Scallops and Shrimp. There is no masking the freshness of seafood that was caught a few hours ago.

The Lifesaving Station has a wonderful wine selection, but I needed to stay sharp when taking notes. I regretfully had to pass on the Cornaro Italian Pinot Grigio, the Oregon's Secret House Reisling, as well as the other well-known French and California wines.

Breakfast
7:30 A.M. to 2:00 P.M.

Lunch
11:00 A.M. to 2:00 P.M.

Dinner
5:00 P.M. to 9:30 P.M.

Sunday Brunch Buffet
9:30 A.M. to 1:00 P.M.

For reservations
(requested for dinner), call
(800) 701-4111.

www.sanderlinginn.com

Yes, I was tempted to eat dessert first. But I'll never be too stuffed for The Lifesaving Station's Lemon Soufflé Cheesecake. You'd never believe a cheesecake could taste so light yet maintain such a rich texture. Jane selected the Pumpkin Scones topped with whipped cream. They have such subtle spices that my eleven-month-old grandson, Peyton, loved them when I tested this recipe at home.

Even though I like to write as soon as I get to my room, when you're at The Sanderling, you've got to walk on the beach before turning in. True, when you're in your lovely room, you can hear the waves slapping the shore, but you can't feel the crunch of the sand or see the stars, which seem brighter and closer than they do at home.

The Lifesaving Station's Lemon Soufflé Cheesecake

Crust

1½ cups graham crackers, crumbled	*3 tablespoons sugar*
	¾ cup butter, melted

Spray a 10-inch springform pan and line with parchment. In a medium bowl, mix graham cracker crumbs and sugar with enough butter for it to stick together when squeezed with your fist. Press mixture into the bottom of lined pan. Place in freezer until ready to use.

Cheesecake

2 ⅔ cups cream cheese, softened	*zest of 1½ medium-size lemons*
⅓ cup sour cream	*1 tablespoon lemon juice*
1 cup sugar	*1 teaspoon vanilla*
3 egg yolks	*4 egg whites*
	⅛ teaspoon cream of tartar

Beat cream cheese, sour cream, and sugar until very light and smooth. (Mixture must be very light so it won't knock the air out of the egg whites when folded in.) Add yolks slowly, 1 at a time. Add lemon zest, lemon juice, and vanilla. In a separate bowl, whip whites with cream of tartar until stiff peaks form. Carefully fold whites into mixture with a rubber spatula; do not overfold.

Fill pan full. Bake in a water bath in a 325-degree oven for 35 to 45 minutes until golden brown on top. Slice with a very hot knife. Yields 1 cheesecake.

3

The Lifesaving Station's Flounder Stuffed with Jumbo Lump Crabmeat

1-pound flounder fillet,
   skinned on 1 side
1 pound jumbo lump
   crabmeat
2 egg whites, beaten stiff

2 tablespoons breadcrumbs
salt and fresh pepper to taste
2 tablespoons unsalted butter
½ cup dry white wine

Cut flounder into eight 1-by-6-inch strips and lay skin side up. Pick crabmeat clean of shells. Gently mix crabmeat with half of egg whites, breadcrumbs, and salt and pepper. Divide crabmeat mixture to evenly cover flounder strips, leaving half at the end without crabmeat. Roll flounder toward empty ends. Brush whipped egg whites on ends to hold the rolls together. Stand rolls up with crabmeat on top and flounder on sides and place in a lightly greased baking dish. Divide butter into 8 pieces and place a piece on each flounder roll. Bake at 325 degrees for 25 minutes until flounder is cooked through and crab is light brown on top. Serve over Braised Belgian Endive with Caper Butter Sauce. Serves 4 to 6.

The Lifesaving Station's Braised Belgian Endive

2 cups Belgian endive,
   torn
⅔ cup dry white wine

salt to taste
1 tablespoon butter

In a medium, heavy-bottomed saucepan, combine endive, wine, and salt. Cover with wax paper and cook over low heat for 45 minutes. Check frequently to keep from browning. When endive is soft, add butter and stir until melted. Keep warm.

Caper Butter Sauce

1 cup unsalted butter
⅓ cup capers
2 tablespoons parsley,
   chopped

1 teaspoon salt
½ teaspoon fresh black pepper
1 tablespoon lemon juice

Cut butter into 1-inch pieces. In a large sauté pan, melt butter over medium heat, stirring constantly until golden brown. Add capers, parsley, salt, and pepper and mix well. Remove from heat and add lemon juice. Serve over Belgian endive. Also good over chicken.

Owens' Restaurant, Inc.

7114 South Virginia Dare Trail
NAGS HEAD

$\mathscr{M}$any doctors suggest that, in order to stay healthy, senior citizens should add purpose and passion to their lives. In other words, they should strive to be like "Miss O," who ran Owens' Restaurant until she was eighty, making Hush Puppies and Crab Cakes until the day she died. That's passion.

Dinner
Serving from 5:00 P.M.

For reservations, call
(252) 441-7309.

www.ego.net/us/nc/ob/
owens/

Clara O was left a widow with two small children just four years after she and her husband, Bob Owens, built their twenty-four-seat Owens' Café. In 1946, they had moved their Manteo hot-dog stand to Nags Head. Purpose surfaces when you open your café at five each morning in order to feed breakfast to fishermen and hunters. Then a smattering of tourists began to come for lunch or dinner during the ten-week season. This one-woman show cooked, served, and cleaned, in addition to caring for her son, Bobby, and daughter, Clara Mae.

Miss O passed her high standards—inspecting every ounce of fish and vegetables she bought, cooking from scratch to ensure consistent quality—to her children. Bobby and Clara Mae grew up in the café. They helped out when needed straight through college. Both married but continued in the business. They enlarged Owens' one-room café to three dining rooms and added an upstairs bar and lounge. Over the years, the Owenses and their spouses, Sara and Lionel, collected the museum-quality nautical artifacts that now fill the spacious downstairs waiting room. Bobby has retired, but his son RV, who also worked at Owens', has started his own restaurant, RV's. He says he took the plunge because he "didn't know any better." His cousin Peaches Shannon followed with her restaurant, Clara's.

Generations of vacationers have grown up with the Owens family. They appreciate the change from a wholesome café to an upscale restaurant that serves Southern coastal cuisine. Not to worry—Owens' still makes Miss O's Hush Puppies and Crab Cakes.

My good friend Jane Brock has traveled to historic restaurants with me countless times and knows every question I ask. We had stopped by Owens' the previous day to talk, but on the afternoon of the night I was to visit, a twenty-four-hour bug hit me with a vengeance. It was either cancel or let Jane stand in. This is what she reported: "My first course was Country Ham Bisque with Crabmeat.

This gets a star, and I think it's because they use Surry, Virginia, country ham, which is not too salty and has that nice, creamy taste. With it, I had Sweet Potato Biscuits with whipped butter. They were delightfully different, with just a hint of the sweet potato. (Dawn, I volunteer to taste-test the muffins when you make them.) The second course was a salad of mixed baby greens, golden raisins, toasted pecans, and Granny Smith apples cut super-thin. It was drizzled with Feta Cheese Champagne Vinaigrette. Who'd think of putting this combination together? But it was delicious. My third course was Pecan-Encrusted Scallops with Jack Daniels Pecan Butter Sauce. The pecans and sauce really made the difference, but you still got that scallop taste. Another star. My last course was a very, very rich dessert that you would have loved. It was Godiva Chocolate Soufflé with Chocolate-Grand Marnier Sauce. I couldn't eat the whole thing. It was that rich."

Owens' says its vibrant menu is "a special blend of cross-cultural foods, served with the warm hospitality that is the family hallmark." Jane felt that was a good way to put it.

Owens' Restaurant's Sweet Potato Biscuits

1½ cups sweet potatoes,
   peeled and cubed
½ cup shortening
2 cups self-rising flour

½ cup plus 3 tablespoons brown
   sugar
⅔ cup buttermilk

Bring potatoes to a boil in a medium-sized saucepan containing sufficient water to cover them. Leave a small opening for steam to escape. Reduce heat and simmer for 10 to 15 minutes until a fork can pierce the potatoes. Drain and mash potatoes until no lumps remain. Cover and keep warm.

Using two knives, cut shortening into flour. Add sugar and mix thoroughly. Add potatoes and mix until incorporated. Add buttermilk and mix until pliable. Knead for a few minutes on a floured cutting board. Roll out mixture and cut with a biscuit cutter or an overturned glass. Place biscuits on a baking tray and cook in a preheated 325-degree oven for about 15 minutes. Yields about 20 biscuits.

Owens' Restaurant's Miss O's Crab Cakes

1 pound jumbo lump
   crabmeat
½ teaspoon Worcestershire
   sauce
½ teaspoon celery salt

¼ teaspoon Tabasco
1 large egg
3 tablespoons cracker meal
3 tablespoons mayonnaise
1 tablespoon butter or oil

Pick crabmeat, being careful not to break large lumps. Add Worcestershire, celery salt, Tabasco, and egg. Mix gently until combined. Add cracker meal and mayonnaise. Roll into 6 equal balls. Wrap in wax paper and refrigerate for 10 minutes. Pat out 6 cakes. Melt butter in a cast-iron skillet over medium heat and sauté cakes for 3 minutes on each side. Yields 6 crab cakes.

Owens' Restaurant's Godiva Chocolate Soufflé with Chocolate-Grand Marnier Sauce

Soufflé

½ pound Godiva dark
   chocolate, chopped
3 egg yolks
½ cup sugar

¼ cup Godiva liqueur or
   Kahlúa
4 egg whites

Preheat oven to 400 degrees. Melt chocolate in a double boiler. Remove to keep chocolate from becoming thick and hard. Beat yolks with sugar and stir in liqueur. When chocolate is cooled, pour liqueur mixture into chocolate and stir to combine. Beat egg whites until stiff peaks form, then gently fold into chocolate mixture. Pour into six 6-ounce ramekins and place in oven in a hot-water bath that comes halfway up sides of ramekins. Cook for 20 to 30 minutes until soufflés pucker and crack and pull slightly away from ramekin sides. Remove from oven.

Chocolate-Grand Marnier Sauce

¼ pound Godiva dark
   chocolate, chopped
2 tablespoons Grand Marnier

1 teaspoon sugar
¼ cup heavy cream

Place chocolate in a double boiler over hot—not boiling—water. As it begins to melt, stir in liqueur and sugar. Mix until combined, then remove from heat. Stir in cream until well mixed. Pierce centers of soufflés and spoon sauce equally inside each. Serves 6.

Sam & Omie's
Restaurant and Bar

Milepost 16.5 Virginia Dare Trail
NAGS HEAD

$\mathcal{M}$y publisher, Carolyn Sakowski, put me on to Nags Head's fun-loving Sam & Omie's. In this, she was not unlike her predecessor, the late John F. Blair, who steered me to his beloved Ocracoke.

Hours
7:00 A.M. to 9 P.M.

For large party
reservations, call
(252) 441-7366.

www.sam-n-omies.com

The loud ambiance of Sam & Omie's is contagious. These fishermen don't just tell fish stories—they have photos of themselves standing beside their 800 to 1,056-pound (and larger) white marlins. Photos and news clippings line the 1946 restaurant's wood-paneled walls. Most of the photos predate catch-and-release laws. That's why the current photos of fisher folk proudly exhibit catch-and-release tricornered white flags hanging upside down on their boats' lines.

You'll like this restaurant because it reflects the feel and spirit of the early Outer Banks. It takes about two minutes to get into the rhythm. After that, you'll just flow with the crowd. No one I talked with was standoffish. And you'll enjoy all the jokes that the regulars play on each other. It's not exactly the Cheers bar from TV, but you do feel a good-natured camaraderie in the teasing. For example, you'll note a sign that states, "Refrain from making loud noises between 11 a.m. and 9 p.m. Your neighbors may be asleep."

Hmm, what do you order at a restaurant with a menu that was swimming in the Gulf Stream less than twelve hours ago? My first bite of the Wahoo Salad said tuna fish, but not quite. The version served here contains a little red bell pepper. Yahoo for wahoo! Yahoo for Sam & Omie's! When my waitress, Margaret, saw my response, she suggested I sample the Scallops. Unenthusiastically, I complied. Margaret, who once cooked on two-weeks-out fishing boats in New England, told me that the reason the Scallops aren't bland is that the fishermen who sell to Sam & Omie's don't bloat them with water in order to attain a heavier weight, as some others do. The result is authentic, juicy Scallops. The customers are the winners here.

The chef uses the same sauce on the Broiled Shrimp that he does on most of the seafood, but his creamy sauce for Flounder proved so nice that I asked for the recipe.

Although I mostly sampled, I was pretty full. But the feeling subsided when I tasted the Banana Cream Pudding. It was so ultra-creamy that it might fairly be called "Fisherman's Crème Brûlée." And it takes a lot less time to make.

Father Sam and son Omie were two of the Outer Banks' great fishermen. When the "unchurched" Sam finally went to services one Sunday, it was an event that changed his life. In no time, he became one of the Lord's disciples. During that period, he was leading a flotilla of thirty or more fishermen into the Gulf Stream on every good fishing day. On one occasion, a fellow fisherman who was impressed with the changes that faith had made in Sam's life suggested that Sam begin the fishermen's early-morning trip with a prayer to the flotilla delivered via a hand-held mike. So, as a melon-ball sun crawled out of the Atlantic, the fishermen gave their thanks for being able to work on the water.

Sam & Omie's Banana Cream Pudding

1 box vanilla wafers
4 to 6 bananas, cut crosswise
15-ounce can sweetened
  condensed milk

12-ounce can evaporated milk
2 small boxes instant banana
  cream pudding
12-ounce tub whipped topping

Line a 9-by-13-inch pan with vanilla wafers. Layer banana slices on top of wafers. In a medium bowl, blend sweetened and evaporated milks with banana cream pudding. Whisk in whipped topping until smooth. Pour over banana slices. Cover and chill. Serves 10 to 12.

Sam & Omie's Linguine with White Clam Sauce

1 tablespoon vegetable oil
½ medium-size onion,
  chopped fine
2 tablespoons fresh garlic,
  minced
1 teaspoon or more oregano
parsley flakes for color

red pepper flakes
½ cup white wine
2 cups clam juice
4 cups chopped clams
2 cups half-and-half
1 pound linguine, cooked
  according to package directions

Place oil in a medium-sized saucepan. Add onions and sauté over medium-high heat. Add garlic, oregano, parsley, and a dusting of red pepper flakes. Pour in wine and cook off for a few minutes. Pour in clam juice and boil until slightly reduced. Turn off heat and add clams and half-and-half, stirring to incorporate. Serve over linguine. Serves 6.

Sam & Omie's Wahoo Salad

1½ pounds fresh wahoo,
  chopped into bite-size pieces
1½ tablespoons lemon juice
sea salt to taste
3 eggs, boiled, peeled, and
  chopped

½ cup red bell pepper, minced
1 cup onion, minced
¼ cup pimentos, diced
½ teaspoon white pepper
½ tablespoon dill
1 cup mayonnaise

Boil wahoo until cooked. Drain water and dry fish with paper towels. Put fish in a medium-sized bowl and add lemon juice and salt. Mix to incorporate. Add remaining ingredients, cover, and refrigerate for 2 hours. Serves 4 to 6.

The Pelican Restaurant

N.C. 12 near Silver Lake
OCRACOKE

The Pelican Restaurant might easily have been named "Aunt Fanny's," after Fanny Howard. She and her husband, Billy, built this cottage in the 1880s. Since Fanny was known as one of Ocracoke's great cooks, it is most appropriate that great food is still being cooked in her home.

Back when Ocracoke was accessible only by boat, the cost of importing supplies to the island was high. That meant that the locals had to be resourceful people who shared and took care of each other. When Billy Howard died in the early 1900s, the islanders built him a coffin. But when it was completed, they discovered it was too short for its purpose. Unperturbed, Fanny waved the workers aside, climbed in, and declared that it fit her perfectly. Since wood on Ocracoke was quite dear, the islanders had to import lumber for Billy's second coffin. The practical Fanny kept the first coffin in her bedroom for the next seventeen years. Neighbors claim that it became her leisure-time retreat, as well as her final resting place.

When renovating Fanny's cottage, workers found an attic full of memorabilia, including a stack of early Vogue magazines. Can't you just envision Aunt Fanny, who was more than pleasingly plump, getting comfy in her coffin with the latest Vogue?

I believe that Fanny would heartily approve of the large, screened-in porch that has been so carefully added onto her cottage. On my last visit, I dined in the evening, but I can imagine breakfast on that porch, sheltered by weeping willows and hundred-year-old live oaks.

For lunch, the burgers, sandwiches, and fresh fried fish carry high marks, but The Pelican also offers salads and grilled fish. New owner Sid Mulzer has introduced an additional dining option from 3:00 P.M. to 5:00 P.M. Weather permitting, you can eat outside at the Shrimp Patio Bar, where diners scarf down shrimp for fifteen cents apiece. Heaters keep the patio comfortable on cool but sunny days. I'm told that the patio is quite popular for late lunches and snacks.

The dinner menu offers a great variety of seafood, as you might expect. Some of the new favorites are Pasta Alfredo, Sautéed Seafood

Breakfast
8:00 A.M. to 11 A.M.

Lunch
11:30 A.M. to 4 P.M.

Dinner
5:30 P.M. to 10 P.M.
(All serving hours vary seasonally).

For reservations, call
(252) 928-7431.

with Pasta, and the beef and chicken dishes. On most summer weekends, you can enjoy live bluegrass or jazz during your meal.

I'm looking forward to a long weekend on Ocracoke, as Hurricane Isabel curtailed my last visit. The island's ferry service was limited then, and parts of N.C. 12 had not been repaired. Fortunately, no real damage was done at The Pelican, and I was able to get some new seafood recipes that are simple, quick to make, and, best of all, quite tasty. The Spicy Stuffed Shrimp is the restaurant's signature dish.

I'm told that many people try to skip dessert today. That's a tough thing to do when the offerings include Cherry Black Forest Cake, New York-style Cheesecake, Bourbon Pecan Pie, and the always-popular Key Lime Pie. To me, missing dessert is like a day without sunshine. That's especially true at The Pelican, a place where those who count calories but enjoy "a little something sweet," as my grandmother used to say, will have to fight an internal conflict.

If you do partake, keep in mind that Ocracoke is a wonderful island for walking.

The Pelican Restaurant's Spicy Stuffed Shrimp

12 slices lean bacon
½ cup cream cheese
12 or more jalapeño peppers
from jar

12 fresh jumbo shrimp, deveined
and without tails

Lightly fry bacon and dry with paper towels. Coat 1 side of each piece of bacon with cream cheese. Place 1 or more peppers in center of cream cheese and place a shrimp on top. Roll bacon up to enclose shrimp. Secure with toothpicks and grill until done. Remove toothpicks and keep warm. Serves 4 as an appetizer.

6 tablespoons butter
½ tablespoon onion, chopped
½ tablespoon garlic, chopped
1 tablespoon sherry
½ cup lump crabmeat,
   chopped

3 jumbo shrimp, deveined and
   chopped
3 large scallions, chopped
3 8-ounce fish fillets of cook's
   choice, cut into bite-size pieces
2 teaspoons seafood seasoning
4 cups cooked rice

Melt butter in a large pot. Add onions and garlic and sauté until they begin to brown. Add sherry and stir. Add crabmeat, shrimp, and fish and sauté until almost done. Add seafood seasoning and stir to incorporate. Put ½ cup of rice on each of 8 warmed plates and ladle seafood over top. Place Garlic Spinach on 1 side of plate. Serves 8.

Garlic Spinach

2 pounds fresh spinach,
   washed and trimmed
1½ teaspoons salt

½ cup butter
2 tablespoons garlic, minced

Fill a large pot with 2 quarts water. Bring to a boil and add spinach and salt. Lower heat and simmer until spinach is done; do not overcook. Remove from heat and drain. Add butter a chunk at a time while stirring. Stir in garlic and serve with Seafood Fantasy. Serves 8.

Beaufort Grocery Co.

117 Queen Street
BEAUFORT

O ver one hundred years ago, the home that was to become Beaufort Grocery Co. faced the water on Front Street. Today, it stands on Queen Street, a few blocks from its original location. This little coastal town was a perfect place to ride a bicycle when the home was turned into Ben's Bicycle and Repair Shop. A few years later, it became Owens' Grocery, then branched out by serving food. It is currently known as Beaufort Gro-

Lunch
11:30 A.M. to 2:30 P.M.

Dinner
Service begins at 5:30 P.M.

Reservations are
recommended; call
(252) 728-3899.

www.beaufortgrocery.com

cery Co., a name that belies the business inside—a restaurant that serves creative meals to folks who appreciate better-than-good food.

Owner/chefs Wendy and John Park refuse to skimp on expensive ingredients. This young couple met when they cooked at the former Eli's Restaurant in Charlotte. It didn't take long for them to realize they wanted their own restaurant so they could do their own thing. Fourteen years later, it happened. They found the location and the town of their dreams—Owens' Grocery and Beaufort—and invested their time, energy, and money into giving the grocery store and restaurant an at-home rustic feel. Like everyone in Beaufort, the Parks do whatever they can to support local products and labor. Local craftsmen enclosed their front porch and planned to raise the ceiling to fourteen feet. But to raise the ceiling, they first had to remove and lower the floor. That prompted them to choose rough-sawn yellow pine for the walls and South Carolina mahogany for the benches. The décor suggests an old sea village. And it replicates the history of Beaufort, originally the site of an Indian village called Wareiock. That name translates to "Fishtown." Around 1722, the town was renamed for the duke of Beaufort but hung onto its "Fishtown" nickname. Historians believe that the last battle of the Revolutionary War was fought in Beaufort in 1782. If you have the time, walk around or take a tour of this lovely old town.

At Beaufort Grocery Co., the food is as rich and interesting as the town. The Crab Cakes look like the usual—until you take that first bite. Served with lemon, lime, and Rémoulade Sauce, they're terrific. The restaurant's Saganaki dish is more sophisticated than most comfort foods. The reason is Kasseri cheese, which has a bold flavor. Brandy is sprayed across the cheese, followed by lemon juice, after which the dish is flamed at your table. Drama may not make it taste any better, but it adds another dimension. This must-have recipe proved a snap to make. The restaurant's salad has an Oriental flair. Among the fresh greens, you'll find sesame seeds and bean noodles that have been stir-fried. The effect is crisp, tasty, eclectic, and imaginative. And be sure to try the correctly named Damn Fine Gumbo, loaded with spices and kielbasa sausage. Besides impressing your guests and family, it freezes well, so that you can pull it out on one of those rainy days.

For dessert, the Pecan Pie is the sweet to order. It's topped with Bourbon Crème and a scoop of vanilla ice cream. Why is this pie and everything else at Beaufort Grocery Co. so delicious? Because the Parks have taken simple foods and prepared them imaginatively. That's the secret to their entire cuisine.

Beaufort Grocery's Damn Fine Gumbo

4 to 6 pieces bacon, chopped and fried
½ cup clarified butter
1 cup green bell pepper, chopped
1 cup celery, chopped
1 cup onion, chopped
2 tablespoons garlic, chopped
1 tablespoon paprika
1 teaspoon oregano
1 teaspoon coriander
½ teaspoon cumin
½ teaspoon thyme

½ teaspoon cayenne
1 tablespoon gumbo filé
¾ to 1 cup flour
2 to 3 quarts chicken stock or water
1 cup cooked chicken, chopped
1 cup cooked sausage, chopped
8-ounce bag okra, chopped
2 cups scallops or fish
salt and Tabasco to taste
cooked rice
parsley

Render fat from bacon in a large pot and mix in butter. Add green peppers, celery, and onions and sauté until onions are translucent. Add garlic and spices and stir for 1 minute. Mix in flour and stir for 5 minutes. Gradually add chicken stock and simmer for 20 minutes. Add chicken, sausage, and okra and simmer for 11 to 15 minutes. Add seafood and cook until just done. Add salt and Tabasco and adjust seasonings. Serve with cooked rice and garnish with parsley. Yields about 4 quarts.

Beaufort Grocery's Pecan Pie with Bourbon Crème

1 cup maple syrup
1 cup sugar
4 tablespoons butter
4 large eggs
1 tablespoon vanilla extract

9-inch unbaked piecrust
1½ cups pecan halves
1 cup heavy whipping cream
2 tablespoons confectioners' sugar
1 to 2 tablespoons bourbon

Preheat oven to 350 degrees. In a 3-quart saucepan over medium heat, cook maple syrup with sugar and butter until mixture boils. Reduce heat to medium-low and cook for 5 minutes, stirring continually. In a large bowl, whisk eggs slightly, then slowly whisk in hot syrup mixture. Stir in vanilla. Place crust on a cookie sheet and put pecans in bottom of crust. Pour syrup mixture over pecans. Bake 45 to 50 minutes until filling is just set. To serve, whip cream with confectioners' sugar and bourbon. Place a dollop on each piece of pie. Yields 1 pie.

Beaufort Grocery's Saganaki

12 ounces Kasseri cheese
6 or more egg whites
1 cup flour
olive oil or melted butter

2 shots brandy
2 to 3 tablespoons lemon juice

Divide cheese into 4 pieces and cut into ½- to ¾-inch triangles. Whisk egg whites and coat cheese in egg wash. Dredge cheese in flour twice and shake off excess. Heat olive oil or butter in a large skillet and brown cheese on all sides. Transfer to sheet pan to cool. Cheese can be prepared up to a week ahead of time.

When ready to serve, place cheese on a drizzle platter and put into a 400-degree oven for about 10 minutes. Remove from oven. Sprinkle brandy over cheese and ignite, then sprinkle flame with lemon juice to douse. Serve with warm bread. Serves 4.

Blue Moon Bistro

119 Queen Street
BEAUFORT

The young, new chefs are hot, modest, centered, and sharing. They're part of the wave of fusion cuisine that's coming to dominate the scene. North Carolinians participate in this revolution when they dine at Blue Moon Bistro. Owner and chef Kyle Swain embraces cooking as if it were a first romance. Every bite tells how much he loves what he creates. Swain cooked at Clawson's when he was thirteen and at Papagayo when he was seventeen and still found time to earn a B.A. in archaeology at UNC-Wilmington. Afterward, in Chapel Hill, he cooked at Savory Fare under chef Gary Wein while getting his master's at UNC. Swain knew that he had to learn from great chefs in order to put his spin on new dishes.

Dinner

Service begins at 5:30 P.M., Tuesday — Saturday. Also open on Sundays, Easter through Labor Day.

For reservations, call (252) 728-5800.

www.bluemoonbistro.biz

In 2002, the 175-year-old Dill home in Beaufort became available. That came at the end of the year Swain took off from cooking to care for his children while his wife put her dentistry career into gear. (You don't get more centered than that.) After the purchase, it took Swain six months to renovate the home. He kept its original oak floor and placed stunning new stained glass above the Dills' former fireplace and lined its walls with baguettes and the work of Beaufort artists. The white linen tablecloths set with small brass lamps give an intimate, yet classy, feel not unlike that of French bistros, which welcome rather than intimidate. When you dine here, you'll hear people raving over the food, but you'll witness little sharing. It seems folks become stingy as they savor the remarkable cuisine, which Swain modestly credits to his "extremely experienced crew."

One crew member works days as a professional fisherman. The seafood served here was paddling this morning. Blue Moon's "Martini" appetizer is served in a martini glass that holds creamy grits and shrimp with bacon slivers and a twist of citrus. Its taste is one of down-home sophistication. The fresh Butternut Soup embodies the taste of fall pumpkins and has a creamy, lightly spiced texture. The Black Bean Soup has a just-right Tex-Mex signature in a chowder body. My Duck with Peach and Blackberry Sauce over Spinach was a winner. The fruit pulled the gamey taste in a lighter direction. I also sampled the thick and meaty Grouper, which lay upon a bed of rich rissoto mixed with corn and haricots vert, which were undercooked in order to keep a crunchy taste. My sample of Lamb was one of the kindest meats that's crossed my palate, thanks to a sauce of blackberry and Merlot reduction. Dessert was a decadently rich but delicate Dark Chocolate Torte, served with Swain's homemade Ice Cream. In fact, every dish in the bistro, including the breads worthy of a baker's talent, is made from scratch. Need I even mention that the wine list is as exceptional and well chosen as the food? Nope.

Blue Moon Bistro's Shrimp & Grits Martini

4-5 slices bacon
2 cups water
½ cup grits
salt and pepper to taste
½ cup cheddar cheese, grated
1 teaspoon butter
8 shrimp, peeled and deveined

8 medium button mushrooms, sliced
½ teaspoon garlic, minced
2 scallions, sliced
¼ teaspoon fresh lemon juice
dash of Tabasco

Dice bacon and cook slowly until crispy. Remove bacon and grease from pan and reserve. Put water in a heavy pot, add grits, and cook until done. Remove from heat, add salt and pepper, whisk in cheese, and set aside. Place butter and 1 teaspoon of reserved bacon grease in a sauté pan and stir together over medium-high heat. Add shrimp. After tossing shrimp several times, add mushrooms, garlic, half of the scallions, and half of the crumbled bacon. Toss a few more times and cook until shrimp are almost done. Add lemon juice and Tabasco. Toss to mix flavors. Remove shrimp from heat when done.

Add cooked grits to martini glasses until they are about ¾ full. Divide shrimp mixture and place equal portions atop grits. Garnish with remaining crumbled bacon and remaining scallions. Serves 2.

Blue Moon Bistro's Butternut Squash Soup

2-pound butternut squash
2 tablespoons butter, melted
4 tablespoons brown sugar
1 medium onion

2 tablespoons butter
1 tablespoon fresh thyme
1 cup heavy cream
salt and pepper to taste

Preheat oven to 375 degrees. Split squash in half and remove seeds with a spoon. Place cut sides up on a baking tray and drizzle melted butter over each. Sprinkle brown sugar on buttered pulp and roast in oven for about 1 hour. When squash is fork tender, remove and let cool. Scrape only the bright orange pulp from the skin and reserve. Slice onion across the grain as thin as possible. Place a large, heavy-bottomed pot over medium heat and melt 2 tablespoons butter. Add onion and sauté on medium-high until translucent. Lower heat to medium-low and add squash, thyme, cream, and salt and pepper. Cook about 30 minutes, stirring frequently. Adjust seasonings if needed. Serves 4 to 6.

Harvey Mansion

221 Tryon Palace Drive
NEW BERN

$\mathcal{J}$n 1791, wealthy plantation owner John Harvey built a three-story mansion with an enviable view of the Trent River. Harvey grew barley and tobacco on his plantation across town and shipped it from his home on the river. He taught his thirty

slaves how to roll the bales from the plantation to the mansion's store and warehouse. They also had to transport merchandise from the cargo ships that anchored at the mansion's front door into the warehouse.

When you enter Harvey Mansion, you'll see the original hand-carved staircase. It's a miracle that the staircase—and in fact the entire three-story house—exists at all today. During the 1930s, the mansion was abandoned, which allowed storms and hurricanes to ravish the interior. For years, there was no one to repair the broken windows that let in nature's elements, which played havoc with the eighteen-inch-thick interior walls and the eleven-and-a-half-foot ceilings. It took a lot of work to put everything back in working order. The Harveys would be proud to see that their old home has been returned to its former beauty.

The living room and bedrooms are now dining rooms, each with its own signature fireplace. The simple colonial colors range from Williamsburg blue to green to beige. Because kitchens were considered to be fire hazards, they were rarely found in eighteenth-century homes. But the Federal-style Harvey Mansion's exposed-brick kitchen with its masculine teak-and-brass bar has become a real hangout for locals. They enjoy comfortable sofas and chairs as they toast the vigorous spirit of John Harvey, who died at the age of seventy-four, shortly after the birth of his daughter.

On my second visit to the mansion, I sat in the upstairs Williamsburg blue dining room next to the fireplace. My dinner began with what I'd have to call the best House Salad I've ever tasted. I mean, it had personality. I told owner Gene Simon what I thought. He agreed, saying, "If there's anything I can't stand, it's a mundane house salad. When I bought this restaurant with its upstairs bed-and-breakfast, I told our chef that I didn't want a house salad that was ordinary. It had to have pizazz. I was pleased with this one." The salad is a special assortment of greens and purples with nuts, tomatoes, fresh red peppers, and a dressing that is neither sweet nor sour but brings out the flavors of the vegetables. My entrée was the signature Beef en Croute. Inside its puff pasty was a wondrous creamed Brie topping the juicy fillet. To this were added Mushroom Sauce and fresh blueberries. Dessert was the wonderful Triple Chocolate. When I think of Harvey House, I'll recall how the chocolates' many flavors coalesced.

It won't take me another twenty years to get back to this time-tested restaurant.

Harvey Mansion's Salad Nouveau

Dressing

¼ cup Dijon mustard
1 tablespoon red wine vinegar
4 anchovy fillets
1 tablespoon Parmesan, grated

¾ cup olive oil
kosher salt and cracked black pepper to taste

Combine first 4 ingredients in a food processor and purée until smooth. Slowly add oil while processor is running. Season with salt and pepper.

Parmesan Crisp Bowls

4 large, thin slices Parmesan   fresh cracked black pepper

Line a large sheet pan with parchment paper. Place Parmesan slices on pan, sprinkle with pepper, and bake at 350 degrees until just melted but not browned. Remove from oven. Place a cheese slice over each of 4 inverted brioche molds or muffin molds. Gently fold along the mold. Return to oven and bake for 5 minutes. Cool and remove from molds. These will be the salad bowls.

Salad

2 heads red-leaf lettuce, torn
    into bite-sized pieces
1 head romaine lettuce, torn
    into bite-sized pieces
½ cup pistachios, chopped

½ red bell pepper, ribboned
¼ fresh grapefruit, separated
    into segments, peeled, and
    skinned
chives and fresh thyme for garnish

Combine ingredients in a large bowl and toss.

Divide salad among 4 Parmesan Crisp Bowls, top with dressing, and serve. Serves 4.

Cake

10 ounces bittersweet chocolate
1¼ cups unsalted butter
6 eggs

6 egg yolks
3 cups powdered sugar
1 cup all-purpose flour

Melt chocolate in a microwave. Melt butter in microwave and mix with chocolate. Whisk eggs and yolks in a large bowl until well blended. Whisk in sugar, then chocolate mixture, then flour, a little at a time. Pour batter into 12 brioche pans or very large muffin tins. Bake in a 400-degree oven for 11 to 15 minutes. Edges should be firm and centers should be runny. Immediately turn cakes out on a plate and garnish with White Chocolate Glaze or Raspberry Glaze. Serves 12.

White Chocolate Glaze

½ cup white chocolate, melted   1 teaspoon Grand Marnier

Combine chocolate with liqueur and drizzle sparingly over tops of cakes.

Raspberry Glaze

½ to ¾ cup puréed   2 tablespoons white wine
  raspberries

Combine raspberries and wine until well mixed. Drizzle over tops of cakes.

Yana's Ye Olde Drugstore Restaurant

119 Front Street
SWANSBORO

*J*n 1996, I walked into Yana's and knew that I wanted the restaurant's laugh-a-minute camaraderie and food in this book. On my second visit, I took pictures. On my third, I imbibed and took notes.

Lunch
Served all day.
Closed Christmas Day and four days in January.

Phone
(910) 326-5501.

www.yanamamas.com

Who knew that owner Evelyn Moore was named for actress Evelyn Keyes, who played Sue Ellen in *Gone With the Wind*? In the fifties, both of us shagged, wore poodle skirts and tight cashmere sweaters, and knew how real root-beer sodas and banana splits tasted.

Yana's preserves a piece of those years. A visit here walks you down memory lane. Customers range from six to seventy. All of them have fun, whether or not they're old enough to remember the good old days. On one visit, I overheard a teen lose his cool, yelling over the music of Elvis Presley, "Awesome! The size of this banana split is . . . It's rad!"

The restaurant's name comes from Moore's Yana Indian heritage. She had me read a history book that noted the tribe's extinction. Then she produced a yellowed news clip from her wallet that proved the book wrong.

Yana's 1949 walls are covered with pictures and life-sized cutouts of Elvis Presley and Marilyn Monroe. Jimmy Dean and Clark Gable rate second. A storefront window sports a Christmas tree hung with Elvis and Marilyn ornaments. And behind this window stands a huge Wurlitzer jukebox that plays Elvis's entire repertoire. Sometimes, you'll see a couple slow-dance or shag like they did fifty years ago. You'll reminisce here while you or your kids wolf down Yana's more-than-delicious food.

At breakfast or lunch, you can order Yana's Spanish Omelet, prepared by your waitress, who'll cook your meal behind the old soda fountain. I did talk Moore out of her recipe, but you'll have to substitute your own chili, as Moore's is copyrighted and permanently unavailable. There are plenty of other options to choose from, too. Yana's Fresh Peach, Strawberry, or Apple Fritters could make a sourpuss friendly, but you may not have room for a Root Beer Soda or a Banana Split. I couldn't chance that, so I shared my Peach Fritters with six ladies from the next table.

I sat in one of the drugstore's original wooden booths. The folks at the tables around me were awed by my Gourmet Deluxe Salad, which stood about six inches high. My cute waitress deep-fried a tortilla in the shape of a hat, filled it with vegetables, raisins, and wet walnuts, and then sprinkled on cheddar cheese and Ranch Dressing. Atop the salad, she placed large scoops of Chicken Salad and Tuna Salad, along with grilled chicken and shrimp. Sliced fresh bananas, peaches, and apples surrounded my tortilla, as did plenty of blueberries, strawberries, and pineapple chunks. To all of this, she added half a pear with cottage cheese and topped it with a cherry. This mega-concoction covered most of the food groups and tasted fabulous to boot. Other diners had to help me finish it off.

Yana's Olde-Fashioned Banana Split is made for two. Partners can eat homemade Ice Cream from opposite ends of the split. Then they can turn the boat around, finish the vanilla and chocolate, and meet at the strawberry. My Root Beer Float came with a brown bottle of root beer. You add to the soda as it disappears—which it did.

Yana's Spanish Omelet

3 large eggs
1 to 2 tablespoons milk
2 teaspoons vegetable oil
2 slices American cheese
2 teaspoons onion, diced
1 tablespoon tomato, diced
2 teaspoons green bell pepper, diced
1 large or 2 small button mushrooms, chopped

1 tablespoon favorite sausage, cooked lightly
1 tablespoon cooked ham, diced
1 to 2 teaspoons bacon, cooked and chopped
2 or more tablespoons favorite chili
1 tablespoon pinto beans, cooked
2 tablespoons sour cream
1 tablespoon salsa

In a medium mixing bowl, whip eggs with milk until fluffy. Grease a cast-iron skillet with oil, pour eggs into skillet, place cheese atop eggs, and cook over medium heat until whites are almost done. Add onions, tomatoes, peppers, mushrooms, sausage, ham, and bacon. Use a wide spatula to fold sides of omelet to overlap the center. Scoop spatula under entire omelet and flip to opposite side. Cook approximately 3 minutes. Remove from skillet to warmed plate and top with warmed chili and beans. Serve sour cream and salsa in bowls for garnishing. Yields 1 omelet.

Yana's Gourmet Deluxe Salad

1 uncooked tortilla shell
1 lettuce leaf, torn into small
pieces
1 teaspoon onion, diced
2 teaspoons tomato, diced
1 teaspoon carrot, diced
1 small radish, chopped fine
1 teaspoon green bell pepper,
chopped
2 teaspoons raisins
2 tablespoons wet walnuts
1 to 2 tablespoons grated
cheddar
1 to 2 tablespoons ranch
dressing

1 large scoop chicken salad
1 scoop tuna salad
1 scoop grilled chicken,
chopped
1 scoop grilled shrimp,
chopped
1 banana, sliced lengthwise
2 slices fresh peach
2 slices fresh apple
½ cup fresh blueberries
4 fresh strawberries
4 chunks pineapple
½ fresh pear
1 small scoop cottage cheese
1 maraschino cherry

Deep-fry tortilla shell draped over a metal cooking plunger until golden brown. Set aside. Combine lettuce, onions, tomatoes, carrots, radishes, peppers, raisins, and walnuts and place in shell. Sprinkle cheese over top and add dressing to taste. On top of salad mixture, place chicken salad, tuna salad, grilled chicken, and shrimp. Place filled tortilla in the center of a plate and surround with bananas, peaches, apples, blueberries, strawberries, and pineapple chunks. Fill pear with cottage cheese and garnish with cherry. Serves 1.

Caffe Phoenix

9 South Front Street
WILMINGTON

$\mathcal{I}$f you grew up during the days when people used the word neighbor more often as a verb than as a noun, you'll feel right at home at Caffe Phoenix. It's a downtown, neighborhood restaurant where you can stop in for a cup of coffee and a homemade muffin at seven in the morning.

Hours

7:00 A.M. to 9 P.M.

For weekend reservations, call (910) 343-1395.

www.caffephoenix.com

It's the type of place that wants you to take your time reading your morning paper. You won't get one of those it's-time-to-go stares.

Nope, Caffe Phoenix is the kind of place that welcomes you to stay all day if you've a mind to. Or to come for lunch with friends. Or maybe to drop in for a late-afternoon drink. Or to finish the day with dinner, the premier meal of chef Keith Ball's day. You can even come to this upscale restaurant in shorts and flip-flops. But the day I stopped for lunch, the crowd was dressed in smart but casual attire.

Six years ago, Nate Hoffman and Keith Ball bought Caffe Phoenix, which is housed in a 1928 building. Its first life was as Mr. Solomon's Dry Goods Store. The interior retains its twenty-foot ceilings and original stairway to an upstairs open loft, used as extra seating for spillover crowds. It's also a little more private and a great place to people-watch.

A few years ago, the restaurant hosted a fiftieth wedding anniversary party for Marie and Max Kahn and their relatives and friends. The restaurateurs learned that Marie was the daughter of the family that owned the old dry-goods store. She and her friends had a wonderful time showing the staff where they played hide-and-seek among the bolts of cloth and sacks of seed sold at the store. The family was very pleased to see how well the space had been maintained and to see the old walls filled with the works of North Carolina artists. As I did, they liked the idea that the restaurant had been named Caffe Phoenix. The building has not literally risen from the ashes, but it was saved from upcoming demolition.

Manager Nate Hoffman has a double criteria for the restaurant's continental wine selection. "You can have a very good wine for a modest price," he says. How did he develop a staff so knowledgeable about wine and food? Hoffman says, "I grow people. We have classes to teach them about wine, about food, and about the pairing of the two. Plus, the staff comes first. That means that they get paid before we do."

It's a toss-up as to whether more people come here for the camaraderie or for the Mediterranean fare like none they've had before. I
was told that Caesar Salad, Spinaci, and Bread Pudding are the restaurant's signatures. My first thought was, How different can a Caesar
Salad be? Ah, but that was before I tasted the Caffe Phoenix version.
The dressing and the fresh shrimp were the differences. The Spinaci
proved so richly Italian that I wanted the recipe. I sampled the Hummus and after a couple of bites renamed it "Unhumble Hummus." It
makes you think you're in a Mediterranean country. Bland grocery-
store hummus has nowhere near this homemade flavor.

Caffe Phoenix is the first restaurant to which I've returned for
dinner on the same day I had lunch there. The reason was the easy-to-
make Chicken Marsala.

I'll never be seen here at seven in the morning, but I can make it
by ten, which will still let me digest a muffin while I read the news.
And there will probably be a few regulars around to help me solve the
crossword puzzle.

Caffe Phoenix's Chicken Marsala

4 boneless chicken breasts
½ teaspoon salt
¼ teaspoon pepper
3 tablespoons olive oil
3 tablespoons butter
¾ cup Marsala, divided

*4 scallions, sliced lengthwise
and thin*
1 cup fresh mushrooms, sliced
1 clove garlic, minced
½ cup heavy cream
cooked linguine for 4

Pound chicken to an even thickness between 2 sheets of wax
paper. Season both sides of chicken with salt and pepper. Heat oil
and butter in a large sauté pan over medium-high heat. Add chicken
and sauté about 3 minutes until lightly browned. Turn chicken and
brown other side for about 2 minutes. Remove chicken to a platter
and keep warm. Add ½ cup of the wine to the pan and stir. Add scallions and sauté until almost translucent. Add mushrooms and allow
to soften; do not overcook. Remove vegetables and keep warm with
chicken. Deglaze pan with remaining wine. Cover pan and simmer
to reduce for about 10 minutes; wine should be only slightly reduced.
Lower heat, add garlic and cream, and return chicken and vegetables
to pan. Cover and slow-simmer about 10 minutes until chicken is
cooked through. Adjust seasonings and serve with linguine. Serves 4.

Caffe Phoenix's Spinaci

1 cup olive oil
¼ cup fresh garlic, puréed
1 pound prosciutto, sliced thin,
    trimmed, and diced
¼ cup fresh basil, julienned
1 tablespoon oregano
1 tablespoon pepper

cooked linguine for 4
1 pound fresh baby spinach
    leaves
⅓ to ½ cup pine nuts,
    toasted
3 to 4 tablespoons fresh
    Parmesan, shaved

Heat oil to medium-low in a large sauté pan. Stir in garlic and prosciutto only long enough to infuse flavors; do not cook. Stir in basil, oregano, and pepper only to infuse. Remove, cover, and keep warm to let flavors mingle.

When ready to serve, return sauce to pan and reheat on medium-low. Remove sauce from heat and stir in hot, drained pasta, spinach, and pine nuts. Stir to coat pasta and wilt spinach leaves. Divide mixture among 4 serving bowls and top generously with cheese. Serves 4.

Caffe Phoenix's Unhumble Hummus

2 cups canned garbanzo
    beans, liquid reserved
⅓ cup tahini (sesame seed
    paste)
¼ cup fresh lemon juice
1 teaspoon salt
¼ teaspoon pepper
1 teaspoon fresh parsley,
    minced

2 cloves garlic, halved
½ teaspoon cumin
¼ teaspoon coriander
1 tablespoon extra-virgin olive
    oil
paprika for color
pita bread

Place drained beans, tahini, lemon juice, salt, pepper, parsley, garlic, cumin, coriander, and olive oil into a blender or food processor and blend until smooth. Use a tablespoon or so of reserved liquid to adjust thickness, if necessary. Transfer mixture to a serving bowl. Drizzle a little olive oil to pool on top in center of hummus and sprinkle lightly with paprika. Serve with grilled pita bread toast points. Serves 15 to 20 as an appetizer.

Circa 1922

8 North Front Street
WILMINGTON

$\mathcal{D}$o you know what type of international cuisine Wilmington lacked in the 1990s? Give up? Tapas.

This restaurant received its name because its handsome, brick two-story building on downtown Wilmington's North Front Street was built around 1922. Actually, the shell of the building goes back all the way to the 1700s, when Wilmington was the wealthiest

Hours
5:00 P.M. to 10:00 P.M.,
Sunday—Wednesday
and until 11:00 P.M.
Thursday—Saturday
(varies seasonally).

For reservations, call
(910) 762-1922.

town in North Carolina. During that period, the building housed the Spanish consulate to the cotton trade. Over the course of time, it went through four conversions, becoming a bank, a mercantile store, a bed-and-breakfast, and now a tapas restaurant.

Before remaking the space, its owners checked to see what cuisine was missing in Wilmington. But they wanted to develop an Americanized concept.

According to the menu at Circa 1922, "Tapas represents a style of eating originating in Sherry, Spain. Tapas spirit or style of eating is to eat by whim, free from rules or schedules." Like a well-balanced meal, tapas offers a variety of tastes and textures that complement each other. You get small portions that give immediate gratification. You choose from different categories to create delicious and diverse tastes to share with friends. "The original tapa was a slice of ham or sausage placed over the mouth of a wineglass and served as compliments of the house," I learned. "The verb in Spanish *tapar* means to cover; thus the origin of the word tapa." The saltiness of the tapas encouraged wine sales. But when the custom went international, both salty and unsalty tapas became popular. Though Circa 1922 embraces these Spanish origins, its recipes have been modified to tone down the salt. The goal is to maintain the tradition of spontaneity while offering gourmet food.

My appetizer was Spinach Salad dressed with a tangy Lemon Vinaigrette that highlighted the salad's Gorgonzola cheese and pine nuts. It's traditional to choose four tapas from the restaurant's selection of twenty-two. I chose Goat Cheese, Marinated Artichokes, Vodka-cured Salmon, and Stuffed Grape Leaves. Each taste was different but complemented the others. For example, the artichokes were good alone but came alive when their red-wine taste met the young cheese's buttermilk flavor. I especially enjoyed the grape leaves.

My full-sized Filet Mignon, wrapped in puff pastry and served over a brown sugar-based sauce, was excellent. The twelve-by-six-inch Crème Brûlée was too big for me, so I chose a tapa dessert of Pistachio Brittle layered with Italian Cream and fruit and served with Raspberry Sauce. It was beyond tasty!

Circa 1922's Spinach Salad

Salad

1 bag baby spinach leaves

⅓ cup Gorgonzola
    cheese, crumbled

½ cup pine nuts

Wash spinach leaves and dry carefully. Place in a bowl and add cheese and nuts. Toss to combine. Set aside. Pour Lemon Vinaigrette over salad sparingly. Serves 4 to 6.

Lemon Vinaigrette

juice and zest of 2 lemons
juice and zest of 1 lime
juice and zest of ½ small
    orange
1 large shallot, diced

2 tablespoons chives, chopped
    fine
1½ tablespoons honey
1½ teaspoons Dijon mustard
salt and black pepper to taste
¾ cup peanut oil

Process first 4 ingredients in a food processor for 1 minute. Add chives, honey, and mustard and process 1 minute. Add salt and pepper; taste and adjust seasonings. Start processor and add oil very slowly in a thin, steady stream. Yields over 1 cup.

Circa 1922's Filet Mignon

1 filet mignon
1 tablespoon Gruyère cheese
1 tablespoon prosciutto,
    cooked and crumbled

1 sheet puff pastry large enough
    to wrap filet securely
6 tablespoons port wine demi-
    glace (available at specialty
    food shops)

Sear filet on a grill just until grill marks form. Remove and let cool. Top with cheese and ham. Wrap filet in puff pastry; bring corners together on top and seal. Bake at 350 degrees about 15 minutes for medium-rare; check temperature with a meat thermometer. Drizzle with demi-glace and serve. Serves 1.

Tuille Batter

½ cup butter, melted
1¼ cups sugar

2¼ cups pistachios, chopped
1¼ cups corn syrup

Combine all ingredients until well mixed. Line a sheet tray with wax paper and spoon tablespoon-sized balls on tray, leaving at least 3 inches between balls. Bake at 350 degrees for about 5 minutes until flat rounds form. Let cool until easy to remove from tray.

Italian Cream

4 tablespoons sugar
1½ tablespoons corn syrup
¼ cup egg whites
8 ounces Mascarpone cheese

½ cup heavy cream
6 tablespoons fresh fruit
raspberry sauce, if desired

In a saucepan, heat sugar over medium-low heat, stirring until it melts. Stir in corn syrup. Remove from heat and let cool. Stir in egg whites, mixing well. Add cheese and stir until lumps are gone. In a separate bowl, whip cream into stiff peaks. Gently fold cream into cheese mixture.

To serve, alternate layers of brittle with Italian Cream and fresh fruit. Finish with dollops of raspberry sauce on top. Serves 4 to 6.

The Cottage

1 North Lake Park Boulevard
CAROLINA BEACH

The first thing I saw when walking through The Cottage's white picket gate was Margaret Crouch on her knees. The co-owner and chef was pulling weeds from her garden as she gathered fresh herbs for dinner. Margaret credits her grandmother—who was instrumental in establishing the herb garden at the Washington Cathedral—as her mentor.

Lunch
11:30 A.M. to 3:00 P.M.,
Monday—Saturday

Dinner
5:30 P.M. to 10:00 P.M.
during summer; Friday and
Saturday only other seasons.

Reservations are
accepted; call
(910) 458-4383.

"Nearly all of my grandmother's conversation was about herbs. As a child, I became interested in her herb research. It taught me that herbs can make even an ordinary dish taste better, and that they are also good for a growing body. My grandmother said that medicinal herbs were important for healing. I know that it was her beliefs that influenced me to cook healthy food." She shrugged and continued, "It was only natural for me to have a menu that reflected what I felt was true. Also, my father was a doctor who treated the ill, so my goal is to keep people from getting ill by eating well."

Husband and co-owner Fred Crouch, who doesn't claim to be a chef, chops and peels everything that goes into Margaret's spectacular soups. He follows her recipes exactly, but the dishes are never served until his wife taste-tests them and says whether to add a teaspoon of this or that. He spends most of his time serving as business manager and welcoming guests to their 1916 bungalow, the former Shaffner-Loughlin House.

The home was built by Osborne Shaffner of Winston-Salem, who planned a wide front porch to give an airy, carefree feel. The gentle sea breeze and the sound of waves lapping against the sandy Atlantic Beach are a bonus. The house has led an interesting existence. It has gone from private beach home to boardinghouse to restaurant. The Crouches bought it in 1980 and put it through a major restoration they liken to having a baby. Thanks to their efforts, the home has received a Federal Point Historical Society plaque and recognition from the Historic Wilmington Foundation. You'll notice the many paintings created by Margaret's eighty-two-year-old mother, Isabella Martin Williamson. She began her career at fifty.

The Crouches refer to their food as "Occidental cuisine with an

Oriental setting," a phrase they modified from Mae West, who said, "I'm an Occidental woman in an Oriental mood for love."

Fred told me that the two soups they can't take off the menu are the Hungarian Mushroom and the Bahamian Conch Chowder. I sampled both and loved the Hungarian Mushroom for its rich, hearty taste and the Bahamian Conch Chowder because of its unique use of spices and vegetables. The key? Cayenne. The reason that their signature salad is spectacular is the Sherry Vinaigrette. The Black Bean Cake is embellished by a lime-horseradish combination that has a sweet-and-sour taste. It's served on a bed of healthy spinach.

Because I grow rosemary in my garden, and also because chicken is always a favorite of mine, the Rosemary Fire-Roasted Chicken was my first entrée choice. It's always a bit surprising to see how much flavor rosemary adds to a chicken dish. I also sampled the Mushroom Pasta, which was so rich that it could have made an entire meal.

Desserts hold a special attraction for me. Not having one daily is analogous to being under-hugged. For me, dessert is as important as vitamins, and necessary for emotional security. The desk attendant at the lovely Courtyard Motel on the beach where I was staying told me to order The Cottage's Napoleon. Margaret's version is soothing and just right. The sweet and tart blueberries and raspberries and the Vanilla Cream Sauce address both health and healing in one dessert. Or you could try her Key Lime Pie with Raspberry Sauce. For the gluten-intolerant, she offers a Flourless Chocolate Cake that tastes better than many cakes with flour.

Margaret's desserts made me feel three times hugged. Kudos to her grandmother for teaching her the tricks of making simple dishes taste terrific and healthy.

The Cottage's Rosemary Fire-Roasted Chicken

1 cup olive oil
1½ teaspoons kosher salt
1½ teaspoons cracked pepper

2 big bunches fresh rosemary
4 chicken breasts and wings,
　bone in

Combine oil with salt, pepper, and rosemary pulled from the stem. Pour mixture over chicken, coating all sides. Marinate in refrigerator for 12 hours or more.

Roast chicken on grill until done. Make sure to brown all sides evenly. Serves 4.

The Cottage's Potato Cream Soup

*2 medium Yukon Gold
  potatoes, peeled*
1 pint heavy cream
1 pint water

1½ tablespoons butter
2 cubes chicken bouillon
salt and pepper to taste

Boil potatoes until soft and cooked through. Drain and set aside. Heat cream, water, butter, and bouillon in a saucepan until bouillon is thoroughly dissolved. Add potatoes, then purée in a blender or food processor. Add salt and pepper. Serves 4.

The Cottage's Succotash

1 cup fresh baby lima beans
*1 cup sweet yellow corn
  kernels*
*2 strips applewood-smoked
  bacon, cut into 2-inch
  pieces*

2 tablespoons butter
salt and pepper to taste

Combine all ingredients in a saucepan with about a quart of water. Bring to a boil, then reduce to a simmer and cook for 15 to 20 minutes. Drain water, taste, and adjust seasonings. Serves 4.

The Cottage's Sherry Vinaigrette

*4 ½ tablespoons shallots,
  diced fine*
1 teaspoon sugar
½ teaspoon kosher salt
*⅓ teaspoon cracked black
  pepper*

¾ cup olive oil
⅓ teaspoon water
¼ cup sherry vinegar

Place shallots, sugar, salt, pepper, and oil in a saucepan over low heat. Cook for 5 minutes until oil is hot but not boiling; stir occasionally. Let mixture cool, then whisk in water and vinegar. Whisk until ingredients are well combined. Yields over 1 cup.

Luigi's Restaurant

1010 Main Street
SCOTLAND NECK

*L*uigi's is located in the town of Scotland Neck, which is on the small side. On the day of my visit, the town had no accommodations, a situation that has now been corrected. I was told that the folks who operate the town's only bed-and-

breakfast had "more than likely gone fishing." The more I thought about that, the better I liked it that they felt free to close their business whenever the spirit moved them. I hadn't realized that the earth was fortunate enough to still have places and people who can do that.

When my friend Jane Brock and I drove Main Street in search of Luigi's, Scotland Neck reminded us of Norman Rockwell's *Saturday Evening Post* covers. For starters, there were plenty of places to park, a blessed novelty to anyone from a big city. We parked on a boulevard-sized street, where I photographed Luigi's from several angles. On busy streets, I wait until there are no cars before snapping away. Had I ventured into a time warp? In Scotland Neck, drivers politely stopped for me to click. Wow! I wanted to hug each one.

Monica and Luigi Cavalieri are the owner/chefs at Luigi's, which looks a lot like my dad's former restaurant in Snyder, Texas, down to its green-and-white tile floor and comfortable brown leather booths. My dad's couldn't claim either the faux-sponged walls painted by Monica or the grapevines with intertwined lights hung by Luigi. This is their first restaurant, though they've worked in the business for over twenty years. Luigi's Sicilian mother taught her son how to cook her native food, which is served along with Monica's Southern creations.

At first, locals were leery. I learned why the place caught on when an eighty-something customer handed me his card. It read, "Ex-Rambling Ranger of the Roanoke." He proceeded to surprise us with a fake shrunken head that looked real. Monica told me, "We don't need a floor show because our restaurant attracts the funniest type of characters. It has become a local characters' hangout."

Dinner was something I wouldn't have expected in a small town. I sampled the spicy homemade Vegetable Soup, good for warming you up and making you snug on a cold day. I had Michelina's Meatballs; the Italian bread the restaurant "imports" from New York give them a unique taste. The best chicken dish I've ever reproduced at home was Monica's creamy, cheesy Lemon Chicken. Though it tastes like you've cooked all day, it takes maybe twenty minutes or so from prep to cooking to serving. I sampled Monica's excellent Chocolate Fudge Pie. And you'll certainly enjoy her homemade Cheesecake.

It's hard to decide whether the best thing about this restaurant is the resident jokers or the inexpensive, quality fare.

Luigi's Lemon Chicken

6-ounce chicken breast
flour to coat
¼ cup butter

½ cup heavy cream
juice of 1 lemon
¼ cup Parmesan, shredded

Place chicken between 2 sheets of wax paper. Pound lightly on both sides with a meat mallet. Dip chicken in enough flour to coat; shake off excess. Melt butter in a skillet over medium-high heat and sauté chicken for 3 minutes on each side. Add cream, lemon juice, and Parmesan and cook until hot and slightly thickened. Serves 1.

Note: To quadruple this recipe, use less than 4 times the cream, juice, and cheese.

Luigi's Michelina's Meatballs

2 pounds quality ground beef
2 large eggs
1 cup Italian breadcrumbs
1 cup Parmesan, grated

1 tablespoon oregano
1 tablespoon Italian seasoning
2 to 3 cups favorite spaghetti
    sauce

Place all ingredients except sauce in a large bowl and mix until well combined. Roll tightly into balls. Place on a lightly greased cookie sheet and bake in a 350-degree oven for 15 to 20 minutes. Or place balls in a favorite spaghetti sauce and cook on low for a couple of hours. If the balls are not tight enough, they will fall apart in the sauce. Yields 14 to 16 meatballs.

Luigi's Balsamic Vinaigrette

¾ cup good-quality
  balsamic vinegar
¾ teaspoon lemon juice
½ teaspoon cayenne powder

3 medium cloves garlic,
  crushed
¾ teaspoon fresh basil
⅓ teaspoon salt
½ cup extra virgin olive oil

Combine all ingredients except oil in a food processor. Add oil very slowly in a thin, steady stream. Taste and adjust seasonings. Yields 1½ cups.

The Colonial Inn

211 West Wilson Street
FARMVILLE

*O*wner and chef David Whitley believes that Sunday dinner at his 1902 cottage ought to be just like it was in Victorian times: "You eat until you're stuffed, then take a nap." That's exactly what my friend Jane Brock and I wanted to do after our second go-round at the inn's smorgasbord buffet. Instead, we rocked on the front porch for a spell before heading home. Needless to say, we didn't eat for the rest of the day.

Everyone in nearby Greenville told me that this is the place for better-than-good food. That was validated as we stood in the buffet line and heard one woman say, "My sixteen-year-old daughter actually cried when they ran out of those Apple Slices. Don't know what they soak them in, but it's good." Every food selection was artistically displayed, including the Apple Slices. You begin with very juicy roast beef that a gentleman slices to your requirements. Next is country ham prepared with little salt, which made it taste even better than usual. But the most unique and flavor-filled dish that day was the Artichoke Shrimp. Whitley swore that he'd created it just that morning, though I'm not sure I believe him. In any case, I found it a snap to make. And it tasted just as good at home as in his lovely restaurant.

The Tuna Salad was very like the one my mama used to make. I loved Whitley's not-overcooked Green Beans and his Potatoes with a hint of parsley. Every vegetable I tasted was excellent. I'd call the food here Southern but sophisticated. It's hard to bring off a marriage like that.

Before dessert, we strolled through a couple of the cottage's dining rooms. Whitley did such a major restoration when he bought the home in 1977 that he received an award from the Victorian Society of America. The cottage had previously been a tearoom run by two ladies. Whitley redecorated his main dining room in colors popular during the Victorian era. The walls are a rich cranberry color offset by tapestry borders. A huge bowl of flowers and some candles dress the original mantel, and a nostalgic antique cherry-wood mirror hangs above.

In a restaurant that hosts folks from all over eastern North Carolina as well as other states, you know that dessert isn't going to be an

Lunch
11:00 A.M. to 2:00 P.M.,
Tuesday — Friday.

Sunday Lunch
Seatings at 12:15 P.M.
and 1:15 P.M.

Reservations are
appreciated; call
(252) 753-2142.

afterthought. If you're a coconut lover, order the Coconut Pie. You won't find a better version than this one. If you're a chocolate lover—and who isn't?—try the Chocolate Cake, topped with Vanilla Ice Cream and Whitley's own Chocolate Sauce.

The man sitting at the table behind us said, "This is one heck of a good meal. Amen." He didn't want to waste time on details.

The Colonial Inn's Artichoke Shrimp

2 pounds medium shrimp,
cleaned and cooked
1½ cups canned artichokes,
drained
2 4-ounce cans mushrooms

2 cups cheddar cheese, shredded
1 teaspoon garlic powder
salt and pepper to taste
1 cup mayonnaise

Combine shrimp with artichokes, mushrooms, cheese, garlic powder, and salt and pepper. Stir. Add mayonnaise and mix until well combined. Place mixture in a casserole dish and bake in a 350-degree oven for 15 to 20 minutes until heated through. Serves 8 to 10.

The Colonial Inn's Coconut Pie

½ cup plus 3 tablespoons
sugar
¾ cup butter
3 extra-large eggs
1½ cups buttermilk

1 teaspoon vanilla
2 cups extra-fancy coconut,
shredded
9-inch pie shell

In an electric mixer, combine sugar and butter. Mix until combined. Add eggs 1 at a time until each is incorporated. Add buttermilk slowly until well combined. Add vanilla and combine. Add coconut gradually. Place mixture in pie shell and bake for 30 to 40 minutes in a preheated 350-degree oven. Yields 1 pie.

The Colonial Inn's Apple Slices

1-pound can sliced apples　　　*1 teaspoon vanilla*
½ cup sugar　　　　　　　　　*red food coloring*

Empty sliced apples and liquid into a greased ovenproof dish. Stir in sugar until dissolved. Add vanilla and combine. Stir in food coloring until desired color is reached. Bake in a 350-degree oven for 20 to 30 minutes. Serves 6.

The Angus Barn

U.S. 70 West at Exit 293 / 9401 Glenwood Avenue

RALEIGH

In any discussion of grass-roots America in the early part of the twentieth century, mention would probably be made of old country barns, Mom churning butter, Dad bringing in logs, children stringing popcorn at Christmas, and the unmistakable aroma of baking pies greeting you at the kitchen door. These are some of the things that today's children read about but old-timers remember.

The feelings of an earlier time are rekindled at The Angus Barn. This is partly because the building is an assemblage of ancient barns and dwellings. In the lobby, for instance, sturdy old log beams blend with the cobblestones covering the floor to create a warm, rustic feel. The stones were ballast tossed ashore from ships anchored in Charleston Harbor. The restaurant's other stone floors were rescued from dismantled avenues in downtown Raleigh. Surrounding one of the dining rooms is a balcony that replicates a loft, complete with hay, pitchforks, and antique farm tools. Located off the waiting area is the Gun Room, which houses one of the largest collections of single-action Colts in the country. And the bar features Wild Turkey decanters collected by Thad Eure, Jr. The over six hundred decanters on display may constitute the largest private collection in the world.

The restaurant's nostril-tingling Barbecued Little Pig Spareribs amply fulfill their aromatic promise. Of course, The Angus Barn is famed for its beef. Its steaks are shipped in from the Midwest and aged for three weeks. The selection includes Châteaubriand, Filet Mignon, and Beef Kabobs. As for seafood, the restaurant offers Shrimp, Scallops, Salmon, Tuna, and Soft-shell Crabs. It also works with Duke Medical Center's rice-diet patients, adhering to the diet's strict requirements for food preparation. And make sure you save room for dessert! The Chocolate Chess Pie has won recognition from the *Los Angeles Times*. Among the other signature desserts are Raspberry Grand Marnier Parfait and Sawdust Pie.

Under owner Van Eure, The Angus Barn has a refreshing philosophy that "the best wine to buy is the wine that suits you best." The wine cellar here houses the second-largest wine collection on the East

Coast. The restaurant has won the prestigious *Wine Spectator* Grand Award every year since 1989. More than 50 percent of the wine cellar had to be dug out by hand because the restaurant had already been built. The Wine Cellar Dining Room has evolved into one of the most unique dining experiences in the Southeast. It offers five- and six-course gourmet dinners that pair specific wines with each course. Clad in tuxedos, the service staff offers silent, white-gloved service that caters to every need.

Before departing, be sure to stop at the Country Store, where the antique refrigerator offers many of The Angus Barn's specialties, including its famous Barbecue Sauce, its homemade crackers and cheeses, and homemade dressings and desserts.

During the holiday season, the gigantic Christmas tree trimmed in the style of the early twentieth century is sure to stir feelings of nostalgia in anyone who sees it. But the architecture and the food make dining here a meaningful experience at any time.

The Angus Barn's Raspberry Grand Marnier Parfait

½ cup raspberry preserves
½ cup white wine
1 quart raspberry sherbet
16 strawberries

4 tablespoons Grand Marnier
1 tablespoon fresh grated orange
   peel

Combine raspberry preserves with white wine, blending well. Spoon two scoops of raspberry sherbet into each of 4 parfait glasses. Pour wine mixture over sherbet. Place 4 strawberries in each glass and pour 1 tablespoon Grand Marnier over strawberries. Add a sprinkle of orange peel and serve. Serves 4.

The Angus Barn's Mashed Potatoes

3 pounds Red Bliss potatoes
1 cup butter, softened
1½ cups sour cream
½ cup bacon bits

½ cup chives
salt and pepper to taste
½ cup Parmesan, grated

Boil potatoes in lightly salted water until very tender. Drain and smash. Add butter, sour cream, bacon bits, chives, and salt and pepper. Place in a baking dish and sprinkle with cheese. Bake at 350 degrees until top has browned. Serves 6 to 8.

The Angus Barn's Chocolate Chess Pie

½ cup butter
2 squares semisweet baking
   chocolate
1 cup sugar
2 eggs, beaten

1 tablespoon vanilla
dash of salt
1 unbaked pie shell
1 cup whipping cream

Melt butter and chocolate, mix with next 4 ingredients, and pour into pie shell. Bake at 350 degrees for 35 minutes. Whip cream in an electric mixer and serve over pie. Yields 1 pie.

Seaboard Café

Logan Trading Company, 707-A Semart Drive
RALEIGH

*S*eaboard Café is a casual, neat place to go for lunch at any time of the year. But if you go in winter, you'll accomplish two goals. First, you'll enjoy a terrific lunch. Second, in order to get to the restaurant, you'll enter through the Logan Trading Company. By walking through this nursery of colorful, aromatic, blooming plants, you'll lose your winter blahs.

Hours
11:00 A.M. to 2 P.M.

Information:
(919) 821-7533.

The café is part of the Seaboard Railroad's former platform, although the green plants and fresh flowers on the tables make it feel more like a courtyard. A high, vine-covered fence almost obstructs the view of the Triangle Line, which will soon have a train serving Durham, Raleigh, and Chapel Hill. If you're lucky, you may hear a train whistle during lunch.

When you eat here, you go through a cafeteria-style line, decide what you want, write it on a carbon-copy order pad, leave your order in a basket after detaching the copy, and put the carbon on your table. Within minutes, a server brings your meal.

My lunch began with the spicy but not tongue-searing West African Peanut Soup. The Tarragon Chicken Salad was made with walnuts instead of pecans. The more I ate, the better I liked this version. A clever idea was the accompanying fruit salad, which had coconut and marshmallows like my grandmother's ambrosia, but also more fruit. It's obvious that owners Rick Perales and Tom Deak taste-test the combinations of foods that go onto the plates here. Each item was in sync, right down to the freshly baked Pumpkin Muffin that didn't skimp on the fresh pumpkin. I also sampled the Raspberry-Dijon Pasta Salad and the Greek Grilled Chicken Breast. I tried to talk them into sharing the latter recipe but got a firm nothing doing. The only item they don't bake on the premises is the Cranberry and Walnut Cookies, which are offered for dessert.

I was surprised to learn that Perales got into the restaurant business by bringing his homemade tacos to Robert Logan and fellow workers when he was employed at the nursery. Soon, he couldn't keep up with demand. When he decided he wanted to branch out, the old Seaboard platform, which the Logans weren't using, was given a new personality. Thankfully, the "Colored Only" benches of times past are long gone today. "I never knew that I was discriminated against," says Perales, of Mexican descent. "I thought it was just where I was to sit."

Seaboard Café's Pumpkin Muffins

2 cups all-purpose flour
1½ cups sugar
½ teaspoon ground ginger
1 teaspoon salt
½ teaspoon cinnamon
½ teaspoon baking soda

2 large eggs
¾ cup buttermilk
1 cup fresh pumpkin
1 teaspoon vanilla
½ cup vegetable oil

Preheat oven to 350 degrees. Mix all dry ingredients until well combined. In a separate bowl, mix all wet ingredients. Add wet ingredients to dry ingredients and mix until incorporated. Grease or spray muffin pans, fill ⅔ full, and bake 15-20 minutes. Yields 18 to 24 muffins.

Seaboard Café's Tarragon Chicken Salad

1½ pounds boneless,
  skinless chicken breasts,
  cooked and cut into bite-
  size pieces
¼ cup sour cream
¼ cup mayonnaise
1 rib celery, cut into 1-inch-
  long strips

½ tablespoon dried tarragon,
  crumbled
¼ cup walnut, chopped
salt and freshly ground
  pepper to taste
20 to 25 white grapes

Place chicken in a medium-sized bowl. Whisk sour cream and mayonnaise together and pour over chicken. Add celery, tarragon, walnuts, and salt and pepper and toss until well combined. Cover and refrigerate for at least 4 hours. Garnish with grapes and serve. Serves 6 to 8.

3 tablespoons vegetable oil
6 medium onions, chopped
1 teaspoon or less cayenne
2 teaspoons fresh ginger,
  grated
2 cups carrots, chopped
4 cups sweet or white potatoes,
  peeled and chopped

8 cups vegetable stock
4 cups tomato juice
2 cups smooth peanut butter
2 tablespoons sugar, if needed
2 cups chives, chopped

Heat oil in a soup pot over medium-high heat. Sauté onions until translucent. Stir in cayenne and ginger. Add carrots and sauté for a couple of minutes. Mix in potatoes and stock. Bring mixture to a boil, lower heat to simmer, and cook about 15 minutes until vegetables are tender. Remove from heat and pour mixture into a food processor in increments, adding tomato juice and puréeing. Return puréed mixture to soup pot. Stir in peanut butter until smooth. Taste soup and add sugar a tablespoon at a time if needed.

When ready to serve, ladle soup into bowls and top with chives. Serves 12 to 16.

Second Empire Restaurant and Tavern

330 Hillsborough Street
RALEIGH

$\mathcal{A}$t Second Empire, even the butter is stamped with the Roman numeral II. The late Raleigh mayor William H. Dodd would be pleased to see details like this used in the rebirth of the Victorian mansion that he built in 1879 and almost lived in.

The mayor chose an architectural style developed in France under Napoleon III. As the story goes, he was financing the home through a loan from his father. When it was nearing completion, the mayor's father overimbibed and was arrested. The mayor could have pardoned his dad's offense but didn't. That caused his peeved father to renege on the home's financing.

Dinner
5:30 P.M. to 10:00 P.M.,
Monday—Saturday.

Tavern Fare
4:30 P.M. to 10 P.M.,
Monday—Thursday;
4:30 P.M. to 11 P.M.,
Friday—Saturday.

For reservations, call
(919) 829-3663.

www.second-empire.com

In 1883, Colonel John W. Hinsdale bought Dodd's magnificent home. His heirs lived here until 1971. Then, one morning, real-estate investor Kim Reynolds read in the newspaper about the home's impending destruction. She had a vision of how it could be saved and transformed into something productive. Reynolds convinced her family to buy the home and restore it to its original grandeur. Its brick walls, heart-pine floors, masonry walls, doors, and leaded-glass windows all needed work. A new black walnut hand-carved stairway took craftsman George Rickman six years to build. And the kitchen was redesigned by chef Daniel Schurr. When you walk into the beautiful old home featuring paintings by North Carolina artists, hanging lamps, and fireplaces that look like they are original to the property, you'll be awed by the authenticity.

Perhaps the smartest thing Kim Reynolds's family did besides undertaking the restoration was making Daniel Schurr a partner. You can enjoy your meal in one of seven dining rooms, which include a year-round patio and a less formal tavern. I chose the former parlor, which has a fireplace and a fourteen-foot ceiling. My first course was the imaginative Sautéed Crab Cakes. It's a creamy mousseline of cod and crab meat with Arugula Pesto and goat cheese, nestled upon angel hair pasta. Another excellent choice is the Roasted Eggplant and Tomato Soup. Be sure to nibble on the bread, which has a slight taste of honey and fine-textured cornmeal. Doctors suggest we eat salmon twice a week, which is no hardship when it's Columbia River King Salmon with a sauce featuring the robust flavor of capers. It's served with healthy Collards and Fingerling Potatoes that hint of curry. This dish is the essence of Schurr's contemporary American cuisine.

You might consider concluding your meal with a scoop of Raspberry Sorbet and one of Lemon-Buttermilk Sorbet.

Second Empire's Columbia River King Salmon with Fingerling Potatoes

Capers and Red Pepper Emulsion Sauce

1 teaspoon shallots, chopped
1 teaspoon garlic, minced
1 tablespoon bell pepper,
 chopped and roasted

¼ cup chicken broth
¼ cup white wine
½ cup olive oil
1 teaspoon Italian herbs

Put shallots, garlic, and bell pepper in a food processor and blend with chicken broth. Add white wine a little at a time. Add oil in a thin stream very slowly. Add herbs, blend into an emulsion, and set aside.

King Salmon

2 8-ounce fillets king salmon
2 tablespoons butter, melted

salt and pepper to taste

In a large cast-iron skillet, sauté salmon in butter until brown on both sides. Spoon Capers and Red Pepper Emulsion Sauce over salmon and finish under broiler until done.

To serve, put Collards, Fingerling Potatoes, and salmon on each of 2 plates and drizzle salmon with additional sauce. Serves 2.

Fingerling Potatoes

2 tablespoons butter
2 tablespoon scallions, sliced
2 teaspoons shallots, chopped
2 teaspoons lemon juice
1 tablespoon parsley, chopped

1 cup heavy cream
½ teaspoon curry
¾ cup fingerling potatoes,
 boiled and fork-mashed

Melt butter in skillet and sweat scallions and shallots for about 5 minutes; stir to keep from burning. When translucent, add lemon juice and parsley. Mix cream with curry. Add scallions mixture and curry mixture to potatoes and thoroughly combine. Set aside; keep warm.

Arugula Pesto

½ cup Parmesan, grated
salt and pepper to taste
2 cups fresh arugula

2 tablespoons pine nuts
½ cup olive oil

Combine all ingredients except oil in a food processor and process until puréed. Restart processor and very slowly add oil until it becomes an emulsion. Set aside.

Crab Cakes

1 cup codfish, chopped
2½ to 3 cups heavy cream
2 cups jumbo lump crabmeat,
    picked clean
2 tablespoons lemon juice
2 pinches basil
2 tablespoons scallions, sliced
1 tablespoon mayonnaise

2 tablespoons parsley, chopped
salt and freshly ground pepper to
taste
2 to 3 tablespoons butter
½ pound angel hair pasta,
    prepared according to package
directions
½ cup goat cheese, crumbled

In a food processor, purée codfish with a little cream to start. Continue to add cream as needed until a smooth but not runny consistency is reached. In a medium-size bowl, gently combine all ingredients. Shape mixture into 8 crab cakes. Cover and refrigerate for 1 hour. Heat butter in a heavy skillet and sauté cakes on medium-high until golden brown on both sides. Finish in a 400-degree oven until cakes are hot in the center. Set aside and keep warm. Yields 8 crabcakes.

Anotherthyme Restaurant and Bar

109 North Gregson Street
DURHAM

*R*osemary, fennel, and spear-mint grow in Anotherthyme's window boxes, which is a hint of how this restaurant began back in 1982. The 1926 brick building first housed a barbershop, then a tailor's shop, and then Mayola's Restaurant.

From the restaurant's current name, you might guess that the interior will have a country-comfortable design. Guess again. The look is closer to that of a chic French bistro. Thimble-sized

lights intertwine through grapevines that hang from a barrel-vaulted ceiling. Cool jazz permeates the atmosphere. Each table is set with a vase of fresh white roses.

Owner, creator, and executive chef Mary Bacon knew Mayola's Restaurant during her high-school years. When Mayola (a feminist before her time) decided to sell the restaurant, she chose Mary Bacon because Bacon was a woman and also because she liked and believed in her. This is Bacon's third restaurant. She says, "I started my first restaurant because I wanted my own microcosm of how human beings should treat each other." She also loves old buildings, which remind her of the unknown poet who wrote, "Beautiful young people are acts of nature, but beautiful old people are works of art." Bacon believes in feeding people healthy food that tastes good. Hence, she began Anotherthyme as a vegetarian restaurant and continues to have plenty of vegetarian dishes to choose from, though she now includes seafood, chicken, and beef as well.

The food presentation here reaches the level of creative art. The lovely, pale, ruby-colored Fennel Beet and Lime Soup is accented with sour cream. Because I often sample many different foods, I try to limit myself to two bites — just enough to identify the flavors. But I ate all of this creamy concoction with a citrus taste.

Next, I tried the Fresh Clams dipped in Lemon Butter Sauce. The warm Chevre Salad with Shiitake Mushrooms and Pecans was perfect for lunch. My entrée — Anotherthyme's summer signature dish, Greek Chicken — was as much of a surprise as all the rest. Free-range chicken tastes the best, especially when paired with cooked spinach, tomato, cheese, and a spicy Balsamic Vinaigrette that makes its own statement.

My dessert, Raspberries Cocette, looked exactly like a big baked muffin. You break the brown-sugar crust with your fork or spoon, then dip down to the bottom and scoop up the fresh, tart berries, which have been mixed with cream. First tart, then sweet—exactly as you'd expect a wonderful dessert to taste.

You can't pigeonhole Bacon's eclectic cuisine. It's Mediterranean, Southwestern, Asian, and vegetarian. It's fantastic comfort food, too. Anotherthyme is a restaurant where you'll feel comfortable but know you've definitely dined in style.

Anotherthyme's Fennel Beet and Lime Soup

½ cup virgin olive oil

⅓ head of red cabbage, shredded

⅓ head of white cabbage, shredded

⅓ cup onion, minced

1 cup leeks without greens, chopped

1 tablespoon sugar

2 tablespoons fresh fennel, crushed

1¼ tablespoons salt

½ tablespoon ground pepper

16-ounce can beets, including juice

8 cups vegetable stock or vegetable bouillon

3 tablespoons raspberry vinegar

3 tablespoons fresh lime juice

sour cream

In a soup pot, heat oil and add red cabbage, white cabbage, onions, leeks, sugar, fennel, salt, and pepper. Sauté about 10 minutes on medium-high. Bring to a boil and add beet juice and vegetable stock. Cook for 20 minutes. Chop beets, add to mixture, and cool for 2 hour. Mix in raspberry vinegar and lime juice thoroughly. To serve, ladle soup into bowls and add a dollop of sour cream to each. Yields 1⅔ gallons. Freezes well.

Anotherthyme's Greek Chicken

Greek Marinade

2½ tablespoons garlic, minced

2½ tablespoons oregano

2½ tablespoons marjoram

2½ tablespoons basil

2½ tablespoons thyme

2½ tablespoons lemon juice

2½ tablespoons fresh rosemary, minced

2½ tablespoons salt

1 tablespoon pepper

zest of 1 large lemon

¾ cup olive oil

Combine all ingredients except oil. Slowly pour in oil, mixing thoroughly to combine. Set aside.

Balsamic Vinaigrette

½ cup plus 1 tablespoon
  olive oil, divided
4 tablespoons shallots,
  minced
1 tablespoon garlic, minced

¼ teaspoon brown sugar
¼ teaspoon salt
½ teaspoon pepper
¼ cup balsamic vinegar
¾ cup walnut oil

Heat 1 tablespoon olive oil in a skillet and sauté next 6 ingredients. Heat thoroughly. Remove from heat and let cool. Place sautéed ingredients in a stainless-steel bowl. Whisk in walnut oil and remaining olive oil in a slow, steady stream to emulsify. Set aside.

Chicken

4 small, skinless, boneless
  chicken breasts
6 tablespoons feta cheese

4 Roma tomatoes
1 tablespoon garlic butter
4 cups fresh spinach

Place chicken between 2 sheets of wax paper. Pound chicken twice gently with a meat mallet. Pour ½ of marinade on 4 plates and place chicken breasts on top. Brush top of chicken with remaining marinade. Refrigerate for a minimum of 2 hours. Crumble feta cheese and reserve. Slice tomatoes in thirds lengthwise. Put garlic butter in a skillet over medium heat. Add spinach and stir until spinach wilts. Keep warm. Grill chicken over medium heat; don't overcook. Slice each chicken breast into 5 pieces. To serve, divide spinach among 4 plates. Alternate chicken, feta, and tomato across plate. Sprinkle with Balsamic Vinaigrette and serve. Serves 4.

Pop's Trattoria

810 West Peabody Street
DURHAM

You might have a hard time guessing the original purpose of the building that now houses Pop's Trattoria. Clue one is the original smokestacks behind the two-story, brick structure of 1927 vintage. Clue two is that the building once held pieces of equipment called hogsheads. Clue three should nail it for you: The structure was built by Liggett & Myers. The cigarette manufacturer used the building to age tobacco in hogsheads.

Lunch
11:30 A.M. to 2:00 P.M.,
Monday—Friday.

Dinner
5:30 P.M. to 10:30 P.M.,
Tuesday—Saturday.
Reservations are
recommended; call
(919) 956-7677.

www.pops-durham.com

After Liggett & Myers changed its method of operations, the building was transformed into a laundry for hospital linens. In the 1960s, the local hospital set up its own in-house laundry. A dry-cleaning shop occupied the premises next, followed by a consignment store. When the building was renovated in 1991 for use as a restaurant, industrial artist Al Frega recycled the former laundry's sturdy old pipes into the handsome railing on the building's exterior. And though you wouldn't know it, you enter the restaurant from the old loading dock.

Pop's has become one of Durham's most popular restaurants. In Italy, a trattoria is a small, modest place to dine. Americans might call it a neighborhood hangout. Pop's has retained the old building's exposed-brick walls and placed an open kitchen on one side of the large room. The opposite wall holds shelves full of glasses, dishes, and a coffee dispenser. Boxes of wine are artistically displayed on the top shelf. Pop's has a casual atmosphere that will make you feel you're in an Italian kitchen. Diners here particularly enjoy artist Jane Filer's huge canvases, which evoke as much humor as they do serious thought.

Since I'm used to eating olives that are cold or room temperature, I found a warm, marinated dish of them distinctly different. I enjoyed that Antipasto so much that I ordered another. My entrée was Pop's Big Bowl of Mussels, served with toasted garlic and roasted tomatoes. Mussels are like peanuts—you don't want just one.

The rich Antipasti called for a light dessert. The Tiramisu tempted me, but the Blueberry Sorbetto and Sangria Sorbetto offered the cool, refreshing tastes that my palate needed. I had a scoop of each and decided that the blueberry was the recipe I wanted to add to my list.

Pop's Trattoria's Blueberry Sorbetto

1 pound blueberries, fresh or
frozen
⅞ cup sugar
½ cup plus 3 tablespoons
light, fruity red wine

½ teaspoon orange zest
½ teaspoon lemon zest
½ cup orange juice
juice of ¼ to ½ lemon

Combine all ingredients except lemon juice in a stainless-steel saucepan and bring to a gentle simmer. Stir and let simmer until blueberry skins split. Remove pan from heat and pass cooked mixture through a food mill, using a fine-mesh insert, or press through a fine-mesh strainer using a rubber spatula or the back of a large spoon to squeeze juice from berries. Taste and add lemon juice according to preference. If the flavor is too intense or the base too thick, you may compensate by adding ½ to 1 cup sparkling water.

Freeze in an ice-cream maker, following maker's directions. Or pour mixture into a shallow 8-by-5-inch pan, cover tightly with 2 layers of aluminum foil, and put in freezer until almost frozen solid. Remove, put in a food processor fitted with a steel blade, crush, and place back in original pan. This is to remove air bubbles. Refreeze and repeat last instruction, if needed. Serves 4 to 6.

Note: If desired, add some or all of blueberry pulp to mixture.

Pop's Trattoria's Big Bowl of Mussels

2 pounds mussels
2 tablespoons garlic, sliced
2 tablespoons shallots, sliced
pinch of crushed red pepper
    flakes
3 tablespoons butter

½ cup tomato, chopped
½ cup chicken stock
½ cup white wine
salt and pepper to taste
pinch of Italian parsley

When purchasing mussels, select those with tightly closed shells or those that snap shut when tapped. Otherwise, they're not alive or fresh.

Toast garlic, shallots, and pepper flakes together. Melt butter in large Dutch oven over medium-high heat. Add tomatoes, chicken stock, wine, salt and pepper, and mussels. Lower heat to medium and cook until all mussels have opened. Garnish with parsley and serve. Serves 2.

Tupelo's Restaurant
and Bar

101 North Churton Street
HILLSBOROUGH

$\mathcal{W}$ hen an ingredient that sweetens comes to mind, you think of sugar 99 percent of the time. Sugar comes from cane, of course, but not everyone knows that it also comes from beets and several fruits as well. Few folks would consider the Southern-grown tupelo tree as a sweetening source. These trees do especially well in Florida.

Tupelo honey is used in a great many of restaurateur Matt Carroll's New Orleans-influenced dishes, even in butter. How does Carroll's type of food go over in Hillsborough, one of North Carolina's early capitals? As the local folks might say, "It's doing just fine." On any day around dinnertime, you can see folks crossing Tupelo's historic black and white ceramic-tile entrance to open the building's tiger oak doors, which, like the tiles, have been in use since the 1850s.

The fine brick building that houses Tupelo's is considered a good example of Gothic Revival architecture. Gothic Revival was the "in" style during the 1920s, when this 1850s building underwent a facelift. At that time, it served as the pharmacy of Dr. Hayes. After paying for the renovation, the doctor christened the business Sue Hayes Pharmacy and gave it to his daughter, Sue. Although Miss Hayes was not a trained pharmacist, her father taught her how to make the medicines he needed. Sue may have considered the task no more difficult than baking a cake and just followed the recipes. Back then, a person didn't need a diploma to accomplish the task. Back then, Dr. Hayes made house calls, and Sue was often seen walking up and down Churton Street to dispense medicines to her father's patients.

My first sample was a very Southern dish of Fried Green Tomatoes. Tupelo's tomatoes are crunchy because they aren't deep-fried too long. Even though it was early summer and the tomato crop hadn't come in, my tomatoes had a definite summertime twang. The soup of the day was Black Bean with a twist—New Orleans seasoning. In fact, this popular seasoning is what makes Tupelo's Crawfish Ravioli, Voodoo Shrimp, and Jambalaya taste so good. The locals were unsure at first but quickly became converts, as I did, too.

Sometimes, it takes a few meals before you become a devotee. For

Lunch
11:30 A.M. to 3:00 P.M.,
Monday—Saturday.

Dinner
5:00 P.M. to 9:00 P.M.,
Monday—Thursday;
5:00 P.M. to 10:00 P.M.,
Friday—Saturday.

For reservations, call
(919) 643-7722.

www.tupelos.com

example, the Jambalaya is prepared with Andouille sausage, which gives it a hotter-than-usual taste. You quickly learn to take small bites and to have a large glass of iced tea or beer close at hand.

It's not hard to identify the ingredient that makes some of the dishes here a bit different. Look no further than the name. The restaurant's supplier delivers tupelo honey in bulk. For home use, you can substitute clover honey.

Tupelo's Jambalaya

2 tablespoons olive oil
1 large onion, chopped
½ cup red bell pepper, chopped
½ cup green bell pepper, chopped
2 tablespoons garlic, diced
¾ pound Andouille sausage, browned, drained, and crumbled

1 cup chicken breast, cut into bite-size pieces
salt and pepper to taste
2 cups tomato, chopped
20 medium shrimp, deveined
1½ cups seafood stock
1 tablespoon Worcestershire sauce
1 tablespoon Creole seasoning
4 cups white rice, cooked

Put olive oil in a large sauté pan over medium-high heat and sauté onions, peppers, and garlic until onions are translucent. Lower heat to medium and add sausage. Cook for 5 minutes, then add chicken and cook another 5 minutes, stirring continuously. Season with salt and pepper and stir in tomatoes. Add shrimp and cook for 2 to 3 minutes. Add seafood stock, Worcestershire, and Creole seasoning. Stir in rice. Cover sauté pan and put it in a 350-degree oven for about 20 minutes. Serves 8 to 10.

Tupelo's Balsamic- and Tupelo Honey-Glazed Porkchops

2 cups balsamic vinegar
¼ cup tupelo honey or clover
  honey

4 center-cut porkchops
salt and pepper to taste
Creole seasoning

Put vinegar in a saucepan and reduce to 1 cup over medium-high heat. Lower heat to medium-low and stir in honey. Stir for 5 or 6 minutes until mixture begins to reach a syrupy consistency. Remove from heat. Cut fat from porkchops and season with salt and pepper and a light dusting of Creole seasoning. Place about 2 tablespoons of balsamic mixture on top of each porkchop. Grill porkchops on both sides just until grill marks appear. Remove from grill and place porkchops on baking tray. Bake in 400-degree oven for about 13 minutes. Serves 4.

Carolina CrossRoads
at The Carolina Inn

211 Pittsboro Street
CHAPEL HILL

The name Chapel Hill evolved from the very hill where the Carolina Inn has sat since 1924. In the 1750s, the Church of England chose this hill, possibly because it was a crossroads, as the place to build New Hope Chapel, known as a "chapel of ease." Over time, the area became known as Chapel Hill.

In 1922, the idea to build a college inn came from distinguished University of North Carolina alumnus and trustee John Sprunt Hill. After a sleepless night in a local hotel, he left his room to walk because "rats chased [the mice] under and over my bed." Then, while sitting under a great oak tree, he conceived his vision of The Carolina Inn.

Breakfast
6:30 A.M. to 10:30 A.M.

Lunch
11:00 A.M. to 2:00 P.M.

Dinner
5:30 P.M. to 10:00 P.M.

Sunday Brunch
11:30 A.M. to 2:30 P.M.

For reservations, call
(919) 933-2001 or
(800) 962-8519.

www.carolinainn.com

He tried to raise money for its financing but ended up paying the entire bill and then giving the property to the university in 1935. When the inn opened in 1924, its restaurant was called the Dining Room. It later became known as the Hill Room. Today, it's called Carolina CrossRoads.

My last luncheon as a Carolina student was in The Carolina Inn's cafeteria. Now, fast-forward to 2004 and Carolina CrossRoads' new décor and cuisine. Blue-and-white-print banquettes line the creamy yellow walls. The Chippendale seats have the same print as the banquettes. Your eye will go to the 1880-vintage tall case clock in the room's center. The food served here today is astounding, which is why chef Brian Stapleton was invited to host the James Beard Dinner in New York.

My first entrée sample was Pulled Pork with Peach Barbecue Sauce. The only thing you taste with some blackened dishes is so much spiciness that it sabotages the fish or fowl beneath. That was not the story with the Blackened Tuna served here, which was appropriately seasoned to emphasize the taste of fresh tuna. Every dish I tasted was terrific, but when Sea Scallops are as fresh as they are at Carolina CrossRoads, I order them almost every time. Stapleton does something entirely different with scallops. Each ingredient comes from the Carolinas—the scallops from our coast and the old-fashioned butter beans, tomatoes, and white corn from our farmers. You'll ask yourself why someone hasn't come up with this combination before. Creations like this come from chefs with imagination. It's a knack for knowing how to arrange foods so that each enhances the others.

The dessert menu rotates at Carolina CrossRoads, which means you may get a chance to try something completely different from what you enjoyed a few weeks earlier. I love crème brûlée and have tasted many variations, but none has proven quite as special as the Sweet Potato Crème Brulée served here. But if you miss that, you may be lucky enough to have the Sweet Potato Bread Pudding.

In 1994, UNC President Emeritus William Friday described the inn as a "grand Southern mansion in its spring clothes."

Carolina CrossRoads' Sweet Potato Bread Pudding

4 medium sweet potatoes
2 pears, peeled
4 large eggs
3 cups half-and-half
1 cup sugar

¼ teaspoon fresh nutmeg
½ teaspoon cinnamon
2 medium stale croissants
butter and sugar for pan
8 scoops vanilla ice cream

Bake sweet potatoes in a 350-degree oven. Remove 2 potatoes while they are still firm to the touch. Continue to cook remaining potatoes until very soft. Cool potatoes, then peel them. Dice firm potatoes and pears into cubes. In an electric mixer, beat eggs until mixed. Pour in half-and-half and mix until incorporated. Add sugar and spices and mix thoroughly. Mix in all potatoes and pears. Tear croissants into bite-sized pieces and fold into mixture. Butter a 1½ quart baking dish or 8 6-ounce ramekins and sprinkle with sugar to coat. Heat oven to 325 degrees, cover pudding with aluminum foil, and bake in a water bath for about 1 hour until firm. Remove pudding, let rest for 10 minutes, and serve warm with scoops of ice cream. Refrigerate leftovers and reheat before serving. Serves 8 generously.

Carolina CrossRoads' Sweet Potato Crème Brûlée

1 medium sweet potato
2 cups heavy whipping cream
1 vanilla bean
3 tablespoons sugar
pinch of cinnamon

pinch of nutmeg
4 egg yolks
¼ cup brown sugar
fresh berries
fresh mint

Bake sweet potato in 350-degree oven approximately 1 hour until soft. Cool, peel, and purée in food processor or food mill. In double boiler, heat cream and vanilla bean until hot. Remove vanilla bean and scrape thoroughly to release bean's extract into cream. Add sugar and spices to egg yolks and combine. Cool cream so eggs don't cook when added. Slowly add cream to egg mixture, stirring constantly. Return to double boiler and stir constantly until mixture thickens and custard coats the back of a wooden spoon. Add potato purée and mix until smooth. Butter and sprinkle sugar to coat 6 ramekins. Pour mixture into ramekins and refrigerate overnight.

Before serving, sprinkle brown sugar evenly over ramekins; torch or place under broiler to caramelize brown sugar. Check frequently and don't allow to burn. Garnish with berries and mint. Serves 6.

Carolina CrossRoads' Sea Scallops

5 tablespoons olive oil, divided
1 tablespoon country ham,
    diced
½ cup sweet white corn,
    removed from cob
1 cup butter beans
½ cup tomatoes, diced
2 shallots, minced

2 cloves garlic, minced
1 tablespoon butter
salt and pepper to taste
16 large sea scallops
4 sprigs parsley
2 sprigs thyme
2 sprigs tarragon

Put 2 tablespoons olive oil in medium-size heavy-bottomed sauté pan over medium-high heat. Add ham and sauté until browned. Add corn, butter beans, tomatoes, shallots, and garlic; cook for approximately 2 minutes until tomatoes release liquid. Add butter, salt, and pepper and toss to incorporate. Set aside, keep warm. Put 2 tablespoons olive oil in cast-iron skillet; sear scallops over medium-high heat. Set aside, keep warm. Spoon succotash mixture evenly into center of 4 pre-warmed dishes. Place scallops in center of succotash. Combine parsley, thyme, and tarragon in small bowl. Season with 1 tablespoon olive oil and place atop scallops. Serves 4.

The Fearrington House Restaurant & Country Inn

U.S. 15/501

PITTSBORO

After traveling south for about eight miles on U.S. 15/501 from Chapel Hill, you'll look to your left and think that you've stumbled upon a Southern Grandma Moses village. Beyond the lush green meadow, you'll see an old dairy barn from the eighteenth century, when this was a dairy farm. The barn, the silo, and a dozen or more recent buildings now function as shops. They combine to make a soothing view for guests of the white Colonial home now known as The Fearrington House Restaurant and Country Inn.

Dinner
6:00 P.M. to 9:00 P.M.,
Tuesday — Saturday.;
6:00 P.M. to 8:00 P.M.,
Sunday — Monday.

For reservations, call
(919) 542-2121.

www.fearrington.com

The huge rose garden and herb garden were producing their first blooms when I made my initial visit over twenty years ago. That was back before the village, which now has private retirement homes, was even on the drawing board. The Fearrington House later became the choice for the publication party for the first edition of this book. History, atmosphere, and imaginative food served with Southern charm played significant roles in that party, which I will never forget. Who on that day would have guessed that The Fearrington House would become the recipient of AAA's Five Diamond Award and Mobil's Five Star Award? This is the only restaurant in North Carolina to have earned that distinction. It has also received high scores from Zagat and many others.

There is something in bloom here during most of the year. Visitors who are gardeners often express their appreciation of the English-style Knot Garden. They understand the skill that it takes to shape shrubbery to resemble a woven knot. Before you go to dinner, take a few minutes to visit the varied shops and to check out the list of things to do in the village. Activities range from golf to author lectures to cooking classes. And if you're in the area around lunch, you can try the Market Café, a self-service deli open from nine to six.

At dinner, I still like to sit in the restaurant's lovely earth-toned dining room. Surrounded by glass, it allows a view of the garden. The menu has gone through major changes over the years, yet the Southern leanings were still evident in my first course, Fried Green Tomato with Morbier Cheese, Lamb's Lettuce, and Green Tomato Chutney. Chef Graham Fox has taken an old favorite and given it a French twist. For my second course, I wavered among several selections. Which one to choose? Cornmeal-Crusted Veal Sweetbreads with Virginia Ham Sauce and Black-Eye Pea Purée? Pan-Fried Goat Cheese with Dried Figs, Oven-Baked Red Beets, and Chive Oil? I finally decided on the latter. It was smoothly subtle, yet had body. My entrée choice took consideration, too. Cornish Hen with Collard Greens and Rosti Potato—okay, I know that taste. But I couldn't image Crispy Bacon with Huckleberry Game Jus, so I just trusted and plunged. It was better than okay, its husky, salty taste entwining with a tart twinge. I also sampled an entrée that paired maple syrup with bourbon and Red Snapper.

Normally, I would have opted for the Sticky Toffee Pudding with Pecans, Butterscotch Sauce, and Clotted Cream. The gooier the dessert, the better. But I saw that the late Jenny Fitch's Chocolate Soufflé was being featured that day. That did it. I knew she was a great cook, and her soufflé proved it.

A special bonus in addition to eating these fairy-tale creations is learning how to make some of them. You can do that by enrolling in Fearrington's cooking lessons. Chefs Kory Mattson and Graham Fox alternate months in teaching some of their techniques and recipes.

The Fearrington House Restaurant's Jenny Fitch's Chocolate Soufflé

Soufflé

3 tablespoons unsalted butter	8 ounces bittersweet chocolate
1 tablespoon flour	(2 4-ounce bars Ghiradelli
1 cup whole milk	chocolate)
6 tablespoons sugar	6 egg whites, large
2 teaspoons vanilla	½ teaspoon cream of tartar
pinch of salt	1 tablespoon confectioners' sugar

Melt butter in a medium-size, heavy-bottom sauté pan on medium. When melted, add flour and stir for 2 to 3 minutes. Heat milk and add all at once and whisk rapidly. Add sugar, vanilla, and salt and stir to combine. Melt chocolate on low heat, cool slightly, and blend with milk mixture. Whisk until smooth. Beat egg whites in an electric mixer with cream of tartar and confectioners' sugar until white peaks form. Fold egg-white mixture slowly into chocolate mixture. Heat oven to 400 degrees. Grease 8, 8-inch ramekins and fill over half full. Put ramekins in hot-water bath with water reaching halfway up ramekins. Bake for about 10 minutes. Remove and let cool.

Chocolate Sauce

2 cups heavy cream
1 cup sugar

3 ounces bittersweet chocolate, chopped fine

Boil 1 cup cream and sugar together and stir until sugar dissolves. Pour mixture over chocolate bits and blend well. Beat remaining heavy cream and set aside. Remove about ½-inch of center of each ramekin soufflé (like coring an apple) and spoon chocolate sauce into each cavity. Whip remaining cream; add a dollop to each ramekin. Serves 8.

The Fearrington House Restaurant's Black Truffle Navy Bean Soup

1 cup navy beans, rinsed
3 slices smoked bacon, diced
1 medium onion, diced
1 small carrot, diced

2 ribs celery, diced
6 cups chicken stock
salt and pepper to taste
black truffle oil

Soak beans overnight and discard water. Render bacon in a skillet until done. Dry with paper towel, then dice. Sauté onions, carrots, and celery in bacon grease until soft. Purée in a food processor and return to pot. Add beans and stock and cook over medium or medium-low heat, stirring occasionally until beans are soft. Purée, season with salt and pepper, and add drops of black truffle oil or similar substitute. Serves 6 to 8.

The Fearrington House Restaurant's Whole Wheat Bread

½ cup all-purpose flour
¾ cup whole wheat flour
2 tablespoons grain flour
1 tablespoon sugar
1 tablespoon salt

2 tablespoons dry yeast
¼ cup warm water
2 tablespoons butter
1 cup dried fruit or nuts

Combine first 5 ingredients in mixing bowl. Mix yeast with water and add to bowl. Add butter and mix until dough comes together. Add fruit or nuts and knead into dough. Cover bowl with damp cloth. Let dough rise until it doubles in volume, then knock back to original size. Mold into desired shape and again cover with damp cloth until size doubles. Bake in preheated 350-degree oven until golden brown. Yields 1 loaf.

Holly Inn

Cherokee Road

PINEHURST

$\mathcal{W}$ould you be willing to pay one dollar and eighteen cents for an acre in the posh section of Pinehurst? That was the going price in 1895 when soda-fountain magnate James Walker Tufts came here from Massachusetts. He found that "the strong pine air was very fragrant."

Tufts had learned what it was like to earn a living when he was only six-

Breakfast
6:00 A.M. to 10:00 A.M.

Dinner
6:00 P.M. to 9:00 P.M.
(Jackets for men).

For reservations, call
(910) 295-6811.

teen. His father died, which meant that he had to find work to support his mother and siblings. His first job earned him fifty dollars a year as an apothecary apprentice. He set about learning the business. In five years, he was able to start his first shop in Sommerville, just outside Boston. Then he began to prosper by making his own remedies and extracts. He also designed and manufactured ornate soda-fountain spigots that he adorned with angels and women. That skill led him to invent a bottling machine and a tumbler washer. In time, his enterprise evolved into American Soda Fountains.

In the 1890s, Tufts noticed that America's millionaires had begun to winter in the South. They built their own resorts, which appealed to Tufts. He sold his share of the soda-fountain business for seven hundred thousand dollars and looked for his ideal place.

At that time, North Carolina's Sandhills region was nothing but wilderness with poor soil. But Tufts saw more. He bought five thousand acres and hired famed landscape designer Frederick Law Olmsted to plan a village resort. Tufts did not build for the rich. His was a place for people of common means. The Holly Inn had all the modern amenities, such as steam heat. No one with consumption was allowed. In addition to the inn, he built boardinghouses, fourteen cottages, a general store, and a casino. Amazingly, all of the buildings were constructed in just six months. They opened on New Year's Eve 1895. Tufts priced the rooms at three dollars a night.

The snug village of Pinehurst is synonymous with golf. A famous Scot, Donald Ross, designed Pinehurst's first eighteen-hole golf course in 1900. Its popularity led him to build three others there. More than a century old, the Holly Inn is a National Historic Landmark. You'll feel a sense of tradition when you enter what is known as the 1895 Dining Room. The pyramid-shaped room may remind you of an elegant English pub. Built during the Arts and Crafts movement, it has soaring heart-pine walls that meet at a cathedral ceiling stained a rich mahogany.

Though this isn't a down-home type of place, your waiter will seat you with a warm, "It's mighty fine to have you here." My meal began with an artistically shaped sliver of salmon beside a creamy white cheese topped by a mélange of carrot and cabbage ringlets. I initially wondered if I should mar a presentation so perfect, but I soon learned that each course here looks as if it should be in an art museum. My next sample was Escargots Dijonnaise, bathed in a rich, warm sauce that invigorated the palate. A tiny intermezzo of Bing Cherry Sorbet proved a sweet idea for palate-cleansing and prepared me for the Dover Sole Paupiettes, an entrée with three delightful flavors ranging from rich to fruity to tart.

Before leaving, I told my waiter that it had been mighty fine to dine here. He laughed knowingly.

Holly Inn's Escargots Dijonnaise

Burgundy Butter

½ cup butter   1 tablespoon Burgundy

Let butter soften and mix in Burgundy. Stir until well mixed.

Escargots

1 tablespoon Burgundy Butter (recipe above)	¼ cup clam juice
1 teaspoon garlic, minced	1 teaspoon Dijon mustard
1 teaspoon shallots, chopped	salt and pepper to taste
5 escargots from can	3 sourdough crescents
	½ bunch wild greens
	½ bunch curly endive

Melt Burgundy Butter in a sauté pan over medium heat and sauté garlic and shallots until done. Add escargots and stir for 1 minute. Pour in clam juice and stir to combine flavors. Add mustard and stir about 2 minutes. Season with salt and pepper and set aside.

Arrange sourdough crescents on a plate. Mix greens and endive and place next to crescents. Set escargots in the center and top with pan sauce. Serves 1. Note: Recipe may be enlarged proportionately.

4 Dover sole fillets
12 ounces scallops
4 tablespoons tomato purée
4 tablespoons yellow pepper
   purée

4 tablespoons basil purée
1 sheet puff pastry, rolled thin
   and cut into 4 sections
1 quart clam juice
4 pea shoot tendrils for garnish

Set fillets between 2 sheets of wax paper and pound to 3-inch thickness. Purée scallops and mix with tomato, yellow pepper, and basil purées. Divide into 4 portions and spread evenly on fillets. Roll fillets in puff pastry and seal to make paupiettes. Put paupiettes, seam side down, into a small baking pan and cover halfway with clam juice. Bake at 375 degrees for about 10 minutes.

Place 3 tablespoons Buerre Rouge on each of 4 plates and put paupiettes on top. Finish with Lemon Chambertin Buerre Blanc and garnish with pea shoot tendrils. Serves 4.

Buerre Rouge

1 cup Merlot
1 shallot, minced
2 sprigs thyme
7 to 10 parsley stems

3 black peppercorns
¾ cup butter, cut into chunks
salt and pepper to taste

Place Merlot, shallots, thyme, parsley stems, and peppercorns in a small saucepan. Set on medium heat and reduce by half. Remove from heat, whisk in butter, and season with salt and pepper. Cover with wax paper and refrigerate. Yields over a cup.

Note: This sauce may be used with other meats.

Lemon Chambertin Buerre Blanc

1 cup Chambertin wine
⅓ large shallot, minced
1 sprig thyme
5 or 6 parsley stems

3 peppercorns
juice of ½ lemon
¾ cup butter, cut into chunks
salt and pepper to taste

Place Chambertin, shallots, thyme, parsley stems, peppercorns, and juice in a small saucepan. Set on medium heat and reduce by half. Remove and whisk in butter. Season with salt and pepper. Strain, cover with wax paper, and refrigerate. Yields over a cup.

Pine Crest Inn

50 Dogwood Road
PINEHURST

As you drive through the towering pines and varied, lush plantings that characterize Pinehurst today, it's hard to imagine that this golfer's utopia was created out of a barren wilderness. The tract was nothing but leveled tree stumps when James G. Tufts bought it in 1895 and hired landscaped architect Frederick Law Olmsted to design a resort for the average wage earner. If anyone could create a pleasant spot out of such a landscape, it was Olmsted, who had designed New York City's Central Park and the gardens of the Biltmore Estate in Asheville.

Breakfast
7:00 A.M. to 9:30 A.M.,
Monday — Saturday;
special items,
10:30 A.M. to 1 P.M. Sunday.

Lunch
11:30 A.M. to 2:00 P.M.

Dinner
6:00 P.M. to 9:30 P.M.,
daily.

For reservations, call
(910) 295-6121.

Tufts led Pinehurst in a new direction entirely when he found his guests disturbing the cattle in his fields by hitting little white balls with clubs. Going against the common belief that golf was a passing fancy, Tufts built a nine-hole course. In 1900, Scottish golf pro Donald Ross arrived at Pinehurst and began designing more courses. The success of golf at Pinehurst earned an international reputation for both Ross and the resort.

Ross eventually invested some of his earnings by buying the 1913-vintage Pine Crest Inn. He endowed the inn with a comfortable, sporty atmosphere that has remained intact for many years. There's some sort of golf memorabilia in almost every room. Today, the inn has newly updated décor. The attractive formal dining room has berry-colored walls, crystal chandeliers, tables set with crisp linens and vases of fresh flowers, and beautiful, comfortable wooden chairs.

For lunch, I met with Mary Kim Koppenhofer, director of marketing for the area's convention and visitors' bureau. She thought Pine Crest Inn was a good place to bring me up to speed on the area. The village of Pinehurst is so quaint that I was ready to move here by the time she finished.

When Mary Kim learned of my love for vegetables, she suggested the Grilled Vegetable Terrine. After scanning the abundant menu, I also ordered a Shrimp Salad. The terrine was filled with eggplant, zucchini, hydroponic tomatoes, Portobello mushrooms, peppers, and fresh Parmesan with pesto oil. I liked it so much that I prepared it for

Christmas dinner. Shrimp is usually a winner if it comes with the right dressing, and the inn's was a smooth fit. Mary Kim had a Ham, Turkey, Salami and Smoked Bacon Sandwich with Provolone and Italian black olives, plus an order of Cheese Fries.

For dessert, I chose the Chocolate Flourless Cake, which had a syrupy chocolate taste so good that I didn't miss the flour at all. The Chocolate Sundae that passed our table looked pretty good, too.

It was too early for a drink, but I had to take a peek at Mr. B's Lounge because it's such a welcoming place. It won't take long before you find yourself joining in the camaraderie that makes Pine Crest Inn a fun place to be.

Pine Crest Inn's Grilled Vegetable Terrine

1 large eggplant
salt to taste
1 large red bell pepper
1 large onion
2 medium zucchini
2 large hydroponic tomatoes

2 large Portobello mushrooms
½ cup fresh pesto oil
1 cup fresh Parmesan, grated
freshly ground black pepper

Peel eggplant and cut into 3-inch cubes. Salt cubes lightly and let sit for 2 hours. Pat dry and grill. Roast red bell pepper, put it in a plastic bag, and let it sit for 20 minutes. After peeling skin and de-seeding, cut into large ribbons. Slice onion into 3-inch slices, season with salt, and grill both sides. Cut zucchini into 3-inch ribbons. Cut tomatoes into 2-inch slices. Season and grill zucchini and tomatoes on both sides. Season and grill mushrooms on both sides.

Paint vegetables with pesto oil and lightly dust with Parmesan and black pepper. In a terrine, layer vegetables on top of each other, firmly pressing each layer down. Continue until terrine is full. Securely tent terrine with aluminum foil. Bake at 350 degrees for 45 minutes. Remove from oven and remove foil. Let set in terrine for at least 30 minutes.

This dish can be served hot or cold, garnished with the vinaigrette or sauce of your choice. Cut into 2-inch slices and serve hot with pasta or cold with salad. Serves 16.

Pine Crest Inn's Gouda Puffs

1½-pound wheel Gouda
1 8-count can refrigerated
crescent rolls

2 teaspoons caraway seeds
1 egg white
1 teaspoon water

Split Gouda horizontally to make two thinner rounds. Divide crescent-roll dough into two squares and wrap around each circle of Gouda. Tuck pastry securely in place and sprinkle with caraway seeds. Mix egg white with water and brush on seams. Place seam side down on a greased cookie sheet. Bake at 350 degrees for 15 to 25 minutes. Cut into bite-sized wedges and serve hot. Serves 4.

Pine Crest Inn's Spinach and Mushroom Salad

1 pound fresh spinach
½ pound fresh mushrooms,
stemmed
½ cup poppy seed dressing
(commercial)

¼ cup olive oil
⅓ package dry ranch herb
dressing
2 ripe avocados

Wash spinach; stem and tear into bite-size pieces. Place in plastic bag in refrigerator to crispen. Marinate mushrooms in poppy seed dressing for 1 hour. Combine olive oil with ranch herb dressing. Peel and slice avocados. Toss together spinach, herb dressing, mushrooms, and avocados before serving. Serves 6.

Ellerbe Springs Inn
and Restaurant

2537 North U.S. 220

ELLERBE

The place now shown on maps as Ellerbe Springs has long been known for its legendary healing springs. In 1820, news of cures for allergies and other ailments credited to the natural springs reached Captain William F. Ellerbe. He came and bought three hundred acres surrounding the springs. Soon afterward, he built an elegant summer home on the property.

Unfortunately, the springs didn't heal their owner's ills, and he died in 1826. The estate was left to his son, Colonel W. T. Ellerbe, who used the home for summer visits and winter foxhunts until the Civil War. That war left many people so financially devastated that they were forced to sell their homes. Ellerbe was among them. Records show that he sold his home and land to Rockingham investors on the steps of the courthouse in Ellerbe. In time, the new investors built summer cottages and a boardinghouse on the land.

The little town of Ellerbe has always been a popular settling place for folks of Scottish descent. Though some locals claim that it was the first United States location for the Highland Games, there is no historical proof. Yet it is interesting that both Ellerbe and Pinehurst tell the same story—namely, that on one Fourth of July, the crowd at the games became so rowdy that the local people requested the games be moved to Grandfather Mountain.

The Victorian-style inn was built in 1906. The home and grounds have been used for a variety of purposes over the years. A crowd of five thousand people is said to have attended a political event here in the early 1900s. The grounds later became a gathering place for dances and picnics. On the hillside south of the inn was a Presbyterian church. Ellerbe Springs Academy was also located nearby. In later years, the grounds proved an ideal place for car races. Today, they host marathon races. While you're here, be sure to visit the Ellerbe Springs gazebo, where you can watch the legendary mineral water collect in its century-old marble bowl.

The restaurant and inn, completely renovated as a bed-and-breakfast in 1988, were later bought by current owners Jim and Donna

Breakfast
7:00 A.M. to 11:00 P.M.

Lunch Buffet
11:00 A.M. to 4:00 P.M.

Dinner
4:00 P.M. to 8:00 P.M.

Reservations accepted;
call (800) 248-6467;
(910) 652-5600.

www.ellerbesprings.com

Lane. The inn's lovely pastel dining room takes you back in time. On the day I visited, the restaurant was serving chef Charles Collins's famous Meat Loaf. Collins has been at the inn for over a decade. Each new owner has learned that you hang on to a good chef, especially when he is the local drawing card. I told him that I knew that his meat loaf couldn't taste like everyone's mother's, but it sure came close. The secret is Angus sirloin ground beef. The perfect vegetable dish to accompany it was the Broccoli Supreme, which was served cold and wasn't smothered by too much sauce. I finished my wholesome, inexpensive-to-make-at-home meal with the finger-lickin' good, old-fashioned Peaches and Cream for dessert. Now, that one could have been created by my grandmother.

The food here is just as Jim Lane described it when he said, "We don't do complicated, we just do good food."

Ellerbe Springs' Meat Loaf

2 pounds top-quality ground
   beef
2 small bell peppers, chopped
1 medium onion, chopped

4 large eggs
2 tablespoons Worcestershire
   sauce
1 cup catsup

Combine ground beef with peppers and onions in a large bowl. Add eggs 1 at a time, mixing thoroughly. Sprinkle with Worcestershire. Work Worcestershire into beef with hands until well integrated. Grease or spray 2 loaf pans and spoon mixture equally into pans. Coat tops with catsup. Serves 8 to 10 generously.

Ellerbe Springs' Broccoli Supreme

2 crowns fresh broccoli
1 cup sour cream
1 cup confectioners' sugar

½ cup or more bacon bits
½ cup raisins
1 large carrot, shredded

Chop crowns into bite-sized pieces. Add sour cream and sugar and mix until combined. Add bacon bits, raisins, and carrots and mix thoroughly. Cover with plastic wrap and refrigerate until cool. Serves 6.

Ellerbe Springs' Peaches and Cream

24 ounces canned sliced
   peaches
1 cup heavy cream

½ cup confectioners' sugar
½ teaspoon vanilla

Drain peaches and pour into a medium-sized bowl. Add cream, sugar, and vanilla. Mix to combine. Refrigerate and serve. Serves 6.

Liberty Oak
Restaurant & Bar

100 West Washington Street
GREENSBORO

The 1890 red-brick build-
ing that houses Liberty Oak
underwent an exterior uplift in the
1920s. It was sometime in the year
2000 that owner, chef, and artist Wal-
ter Fancourt took up residence here.
After twenty-five years in the restaurant business, Fancourt knew what
he wanted and let interior designer Gene Cline carry through with it.

You'll do a double-take when you
arrive at the restaurant, located in the
heart of Greensboro's historic district.
Historic? You've got to be kidding.
The open courtyard—featuring green
umbrella tables and extremely contem-

Lunch
11:30 A.M. to 2:00 P.M.
Monday—Friday.

Dinner
5:30 P.M. to 9:30 P.M.
Monday—Thursday.
Dinner until 10:00 P.M.
Friday and Saturday.

Reservations are
appreciated.
(336) 273-7057.

porary red and blue statuary lent to the restaurant for a year as part of
Greensboro's Arts Grant—suggests a certain *joie de vivre*. Step inside
and the first thing you'll notice is one of Fancourt's paintings opposite
the bar. It defines the restaurant's tone. As Fancourt says, "I guess you
could call my paintings 'contemporary folk.' I didn't want this restaurant to look stodgy, just a place where you come hoping to have fun."
And indeed you do, in an elegant setting.

In the main lower dining room, cool jazz caught my ear, Greensboro artist Denise Dodge's huge impressionistic canvas of people
dining caught my eye, and the Melted Brie topped with Sweetened
Walnuts captured my taste buds. What you may like best about this
recipe is that it's quick and easy to make. I checked out a couple of
the entrées. The Lamb is prepared in such a way that even those who
aren't lamb devotees will like it. I love scallops no matter how they are
prepared, but Liberty Oak's Curried Scallops with mango in a sweet-
and-sour sauce is as innovative as it is good. The impressive wine list
features good Australian Chardonnays and Pinot Noirs and a terrific
selection from California's better wineries.

I asked my waitperson which of the desserts was the favorite, and
she brought me a thick slice of Chocolate Bourbon Pecan Pie. Nothing ever tastes as good as those Mars bars you scarfed down at the
Saturday movies when you were a kid, but this rich, rich pie comes
dangerously close.

Liberty Oak's Chocolate Bourbon Pecan Pie

Crust

⅓ cup cocoa powder
½ cup powdered sugar

1½ cups graham cracker
  crumbs
½ cup butter, melted

Combine ingredients in a medium-sized bowl and press into a 10- to 12-inch springform pan. Bake in a 325-degree oven for 7 to 10 minutes.

Filling

1 pound butter
3 cups chocolate chips
7 large eggs
16-ounce box light brown
  sugar

½ cup light corn syrup
1 cup pecans, chopped
⅛ cup bourbon
1 tablespoon vanilla

Melt butter and chocolate chips in a double boiler; mix well. In a large bowl, beat eggs 1 at a time, adding remaining ingredients and chocolate mixture, mixing to incorporate. Pour into crust and bake in a 350-degree oven for 45 to 60 minutes until pie has risen and puled away from sides. (There might be some cracks in filling when done.) Yields 1 pie.

Liberty Oak's Curried Scallops

Curry Oil

½ cup fresh ginger, chopped
5 tablespoons plus 1 teaspoon
  fresh garlic, smashed
5 tablespoons plus 1 teaspoon
  shallots, chopped
zest of ½ lime
2⅔ tablespoons yellow
  curry powder
3 tablespoons red curry
  powder
1⅛ teaspoons turmeric

1⅛ teaspoons cumin
1⅛ teaspoons coriander
1⅛ teaspoons Chinese five-
  spice powder
1 teaspoon salt
2⅔ cups peanut or salad oil
2 tablespoons cilantro, chopped
2 tablespoons fresh basil,
  chopped
¼ cup water

In a medium-sized saucepan, bring all ingredients except cilantro, basil, and water to a simmer over medium heat. Reduce heat to a low boil for 20 minutes, stirring occasionally. Stir in cilantro and basil and cook for 2 minutes. Turn off heat and let sit for 2 minutes, then add water and mix thoroughly for 1 minute. Allow to cool in pan, then strain mixture through a fine sieve. Do not force it through, but allow it to drip slowly.

Scallops

2 cups sea scallops
½ cup corn
½ cup tomato, diced
½ cup mango, diced
¼ cup red bell pepper, diced
½ cup cream

juice of 1 lime
salt and pepper to taste
cooked rice for 8
fried noodles for garnish
cilantro for garnish
fresh basil for garnish

Heat 3 tablespoons Curry Oil in a large sauté pan. Add scallops and sauté until golden brown. Add corn, tomatoes, mango, and red bell peppers. Cook for 1 minute, then add cream, lime juice, and salt and pepper. Cook on high for 2 minutes, stirring frequently. Divide rice among 8 plates. Put scallops mixture on top of rice and garnish with fried noodles, cilantro, and basil. Serves 8.

Undercurrent Restaurant

600 South Elm Street
GREENSBORO

ike many hundred-year-old buildings, the handsome 1903 brick structure that houses the Undercurrent Restaurant has been home to many businesses—some more colorful than others. Jack Wagner is a regular at Undercurrent. When he was a youngster the building included a hotel, and he delivered newspapers to its longtime guests. Wagner, always a Southern gentleman, explained that the enterprise was a hotel "and then some." It seems that the hotel's clientele included ladies of the night. "It used to make my Mama so mad that she'd yank me away when a newspaper customer would wave like she knew me real good," Wagner recalled. "At 12, I didn't fully understand Mama doing that."

The ground floor initially housed a furniture store and undertaking business, then a general store. During the Great Depression, little cash changed hands. Bartering was commonplace. A person could bring in small livestock and trade for food or housewares and the like. In 1936 a tornado tore off the third floor. Attempts to replace the third level were stymied by a shortage of funds. Instead, the second floor eventually was converted into apartments that have been updated while carefully retaining the craftsmanship of previous eras.

During the past twenty years or so the ground floor has been home to a variety of restaurants. The most recent, Undercurrent, is owned by Ben Roberts. Like the building, Roberts has had a varied life. With a double major in industrial psychology and business administration, his first job was as an accountant. Next he studied classical French cooking at the L'Academie de Cuisine. After working in many restaurants, he wanted to create his own. "I wanted a space that was the right size for preparing food, that would be right for service, and that would have the right ambiance," he says. "I walked into this building and knew this was it."

Roberts now plays more of a managerial role, leaving the daily practice of culinary art to chef Chris Wishart.

And art it is. My appetizer was a Terrine of Dutch Confit and Foie

Lunch
11:30 A.M. to 2:00 P.M.
Tuesday—Friday.

Dinner
6:00 P.M. to 9:00 P.M.
Tuesday—Thursday.

6:00 P.M. to 9:30 P.M.
Friday—Saturday.

For reservations call
(336) 370-1266.

www.undercurrent
restaurant.com

Gras with seared, rare Yellowfin Tuna served with Greens tossed in Balsamic Vinegar. It was sauced in a red wine reduction, and a bit of Dijon dotted my plate. To capture the experience, slide each bite across the Dijon and back through the sauce to let the flavors merge. Now that's a taste to please even the most sophisticated palate.

Undercurrent's ambiance is equally chic. The eighteen-foot-high ceilings and spare, modern décor give the restaurant a cosmopolitan flair matched by the cool, unobtrusive jazz playing in the background.

My entrée was Pan-Seared Sea Scallops Sautéed with Potatoes, plus Apple-Wood Bacon and Onions caramelized to serve with a rich Bordelaise sauce. The presentation was prize-winning, and it tasted even better. One would be hard put to find food more flavorful than Roberts's "American Contemporary Cuisine."

I closed my eyes while tasting the dessert of Grand Marnier Marinated Berries with Sabayon Sauce and Whipped Cream. Summer berries with their sassy taste, embellished by liqueur and dollops of sauce, were delicious. I also sampled White Chocolate Brown Sugar Pudding, an unusual combination that explains why we love to go to restaurants of this sort.

Roberts has made his vision of a stylish restaurant serving top-flight cuisine a reality. A restaurant's setting may not actually make food taste better, but each element at Undercurrent evokes a sensory response; combined, they become psychologically powerful.

Undercurrent's Grand Marnier Marinated Berries with Champagne Sabayon

2 pints fresh strawberries, tops removed
1 pint fresh raspberries
1 pint fresh blackberries

1 pint fresh blueberries
¼ cup sugar
¼ cup Grand Marnier

Place all the berries in a large mixing bowl; coat with the sugar and Grand Marnier. Gently toss the berries to soak up sugar and Grand Marnier.

Champagne Sabayon

5 large eggs yolks
¼ cup sugar

½ cup champagne
¼ cup orange juice

Place all sabayon ingredients in a mixing bowl that will fit over a pot to make a double broiler. Using a large whisk, whisk all the ingredients together and place over simmering water. Cook for about 10 minutes until the mixture triples in volume and lies out in ribbons when falling.

Place the berries in a brûlée ramekin or another flat and open-faced container. Pour the sabayon over the berries. Slightly brown the sabayon with a brûlée torch, or under the broiler for about 2 minutes. Top with whipped cream and fresh mint. Garnish with flat sweet cookies. Serves 4.

Undercurrent's Almond Bread Pudding

2 cups heavy cream
1 cup brown sugar
8 ounces white chocolate
2 to 4 cups French bread,
  chopped
3 whole eggs

1 cup toasted almonds
2 to 3 ounces caramel sauce
1 cup whipped cream, or
  crème anglaise
6 sprigs fresh mint leaves

Preheat oven to 350 degrees. Place a large, heavy saucepan on stove set at medium. Add cream and brown sugar and stir to incorporate. Add white chocolate and stir until it melts and blends. Reduce heat to low and add the bread. (There should be a little liquid left after addition of bread.) Turn off heat and allow mixture to remain in pan; stir every 5 minutes for 20 total minutes. Add eggs, one at a time, and stir until fully incorporated. Add almonds and stir. Spoon mixture into 6 ramekins and place on a sheet tray. Bake in oven for 20 to 25 minutes. Remove and cool. Remove ramekins and refrigerate or serve warm. Garnish with homemade or commercial caramel sauce and whipped cream or crème anglaise. Dress with mint. Serves 6.

Southern Roots

1108 North Main Street
Located in the John H. Adams Inn
HIGH POINT

he roots of this unique restaurant spread throughout the dining room, the intimate dining niches, and the patio with its European flair. Originally, this was John H. Adams's 1908 Italian Renaissance Revival mansion. My grandmother would have taken one look at this magnificent home and said, "Whew, those people had money!" They did indeed. The family fortune came from John Adams's pioneering efforts in manufacturing hosiery with his Adams-Millis Corporation. Later, when the generous Mrs. Adams wanted a larger home, she gave the mansion to High Point's YWCA, which preserved its patterned wood floors, pressed-tin molding, gigantic bathrooms, and six bedrooms. The house later served as a funeral home. Today, visitors come for lunch and dinner at Southern Roots, as well as to stay in one of the John H. Adams Inn's beautifully renovated bedrooms. Elegant is too skimpy a word to characterize the experience. And that's without even describing the food.

Lunch
11:30 A.M. to 2:00 P.M.

Dinner
5:30 P.M. to 9:00 P.M.

For reservations call
(336) 882-5570.

www.jhadamsinn.com

Chef Lisa Hawley creates dishes incorporating typical Southern ingredients, such as fried okra, in a cuisine she calls New American Southern Cuisine. My dinner had to be a sampling mission, as Hawley produced dish after dish for me to taste. Everything she does is a labor of love. Choosing which recipes to publish was a real challenge! Was the Sea Bass with Fresh Spinach and Fried Okra sauced with Smoked Tomatoes and served with Basil Relish tastier than the Lowcountry Stone-Ground Grits with Ham? These are Southern comfort foods, but not overcooked or packing too many calories. Do I pick Hawley's juicy and tender Beef Tenderloin, served with fresh Organic Beans, Potatoes, and Vidalia onions? Or should it be her spicy Fried Oysters with sweet and perky Watermelon and Mango Salsa? Her free-range chicken with Prosciutto, Basil, and Sun-Dried Tomatoes is a new taste in Southern food, and her desserts are wickedly clever. Who but the inventive Hawley would combine strips of Coconut, Lime, and Orange Sorbet with cream cheese? Technique can be taught, but not art. Hawley is an artist who happens to be a chef.

Dine at Southern Roots and savor Chef Hawley's new comfort foods. It's the perfect prelude to a night of rest and relaxation at the

Southern Roots' Organic Greens, Brie, Spicy Pecans, and Granny Smith Dressing

2 cups organic greens, washed   *6 ounces Brie, cut bite-size*

Tear greens into bite-size pieces and place equally in 4 salad plates. Cut cheese into bite-size pieces and sprinkle equal amounts on top of the greens.

Spicy Pecans

3 tablespoons butter   *20 to 25 whole pecans*
3 tablespoons sugar

Put butter in a large skillet on medium-low heat. Add sugar and caramelize, stirring constantly, until mixture turns brown. Remove from heat and add pecans to skillet. Coat both sides of the pecans and remove to a sheet of parchment or wax paper and let dry.

Granny Smith Dressing

1 large Granny Smith apple,   *¾ cup canola oil*
   peeled   *juice of 1 large lemon, or 2 small*
¾ cup sugar   *¼ to ½ teaspoon salt*

Cut apple in chunks and put into a food processor. Add sugar and process until pureed. Very slowly pour oil into dressing, continuing to process. Add ¼ teaspoon salt, and taste. Add additional salt if needed. Yields about 2 cups.

Sprinkle dry pecans equally between bowls and drizzle with dressing. Serves 4.

Southern Roots' Apple Cake

5 cups peeled apples, cubed   *½ teaspoon salt*
2 cups sugar   *2 teaspoons soda*
1 cup coarsely chopped pecans   *1 cup, plus 3 tablespoons*
3 cups plain flour   *vegetable oil*
½ teaspoon cinnamon   *1 tablespoon vanilla*
½ teaspoon nutmeg   *2 large eggs, beaten*

Mix apples, sugar and nuts together; let stand for 1 hour. Sift flour, cinnamon, nutmeg, salt, and soda together; add to apple mixture alternating with oil, vanilla, and eggs. Pour batter into a greased, heavy tube pan. Bake at 350 degrees for 1 hour and 15 minutes. Wrap in foil to keep moist.

Caramel Frosting

¾ cup butter

1 cup packed brown sugar

½ cup, plus 3 tablespoons milk

1¾ to 2 cups confectioners' sugar

Melt butter in a heavy 8-inch skillet; add brown sugar and cook over low heat, stirring constantly for 2 minutes. Add milk, raise heat, and stir until mixture comes to a boil. Remove from heat and cool. Put mixture into a food processor and add confectioners' sugar gradually until it becomes thick enough to spread. Spread over entire cake. Yields 1 cake.

Southern Roots' Blue Cheese Chicken

1 cup blue cheese

1 cup cream cheese

4 chicken breasts

1 teaspoon fresh sage, chopped

1 teaspoon fresh rosemary, chopped

salt and pepper to taste

2 to 3 tablespoons olive oil

Unwrap cheeses and allow them to soften for about an hour. In a medium-size bowl mix cheeses together thoroughly. Lift skin from chicken breasts and stuff with cheese mixture. Sprinkle chicken on all sides with sage, rosemary and salt and pepper to taste. Pour about 2 tablespoons of oil into a large cast iron skillet (if available) and heat until hot. Put chicken breasts in skillet and sear on all sides. Put chicken breasts on a tray and place in a 425-degree oven for 25 minutes. Serves 4.

Henry F. Shaffner House and Restaurant

150 South Marshall Street

WINSTON-SALEM

$\mathcal{W}$ hen I started writing about historic restaurants some twenty-plus years ago, the food was generally excellent for the times. Now standards are even higher. Shaffner House, a gorgeous Queen Anne-style mansion that is a bed-and-breakfast as well as a restaurant, exemplifies today's standards of excellence.

Dinner
5:00 P.M. to 9:00 P.M.

For reservations, cal
(800) 7952-2256;
(336) 777-0052.

www.shaffnerhouse.com

Henry Shaffner was born into money in the 1860s and educated in the fine arts and finance. His civic-minded, philanthropic parents also taught him by example. The evidence of his upbringing is seen throughout this magnificently restored mansion, which is a quietly elegant place to stay and is one of Winston-Salem's best places for dinner. On your way to dine and before retiring for the night, check out the rich tiger oak in the wainscoting, doors, and other woodwork. That tiger oak brought back fond memories of my grandmother's bedroom furniture.

We revere excellent workmanship from the past, and Shaffner did the same nearly 100 years ago. Take a close look at the carved wooden mantel in the original family dining room. Silver plaques inscribed "1776-1907" date the mantel's columns. Workmen salvaged them from a log cabin that had sheltered the men building the Moravian village now called Old Salem. Shaffner saved these hand-hewn columns, which had been slated for demolition, and put them in a place of honor in his mansion.

My friend Jane Brock and I sat on the original wraparound porch, now glassed-in. At sunset the view of Winston-Salem is positively artistic. Jane munched on hot, delicious Moravian Love Feast and Pumpkin-Seed Buns until our Baked Brie, sauced with Balsamic Vinegar Syrup, arrived. Slices of Granny Smith Apple, Orange, Strawberries, and Blueberries also were drizzled with this divine syrup. The quintessential "sweet-sour" effect makes this a sumptuous appetizer.

While I was making notes, I caught Jane sneaking bite after bite of my mashed potatoes (her comfort food). They came with the restaurant's signature dish, Filet Mignon with Gorgonzola Pancetta Butter. I was raised on a ranch in Texas and consider this beef entrée my comfort food.

I asked Chef Bargoil what he did to achieve such delicious mashed potatoes and hearty, tender beef. He replied, "Simplicity makes comfort food what it is." His secret: Undercook Idaho potatoes to bring out a fuller, creamier potato taste. I never ask for steak recipes, because so much of a home cook's success depends on the quality of the beef; but after talking with Bargoil, I did want this steak for this book.

For dessert, Jane had just-baked Lemon Meringue Pie, which both of us found to be more lemony than most. Bargoil kindly gave me that recipe as well. Shaffner House's menu is evenly balanced with Salmon, Grouper, Pork Tenderloin, Pasta, Chicken Medallions, and Shrimp Scampi.

At evening's end, we climbed the stairs to our luxurious room featuring a fireplace, dressing room, and spacious bathroom. We smiled, knowing we'd stop at Shaffners's every time we came to Winston-Salem.

Shaffner's Baked Brie

4-ounce wedge of brie
3 cups aged balsamic vinegar

2 tablespoons brown sugar
fresh-cut seasonal fruit

Bring brie to room temperature. Bake brie at 400-degrees for 5 minutes. Pour vinegar into a medium-sized saucepan set to low simmer. Stir occasionally until vinegar is reduced to 1 cup. Add sugar and stir until it dissolves. Remove from heat and let cool. Drizzle ⅛ cup on each serving plate. Cut brie into 4 slices and place atop sauce. Surround brie with fruit. Serves 4.

Shaffner's Filet Mignon with Gorgonzola Pancetta Butter

¼ pound of pancetta, cooked
¼ pound Gorgonzola cheese

½ cup unsalted butter
10 8-ounce center-cut filets
of certified Angus Beef®

Cook pancetta until done; dry on a paper towel. Crumble pancetta to a fine texture. Mix pancetta with butter and cheese until well blended. Pour mixture onto a piece of plastic wrap and roll into a log with a diameter of approximately 1½ inches. Chill 3 to 4 hours. Cut butter into approximately ½-inch slices and top filet. Broil filets until done to desired tastes. Serves 10.

Note: The key to this steak is certified Angus Beef.® In addition, you may use leftover butter combination on fresh, cooked vegetables.

1 tablespoon flour
1 tablespoon corn starch
1½ cups sugar
dash of salt
4 large eggs
⅓ cup milk

¼ cup melted butter
2 teaspoons grated lemon rind
¼ cup lemon juice
¼ teaspoon vanilla
1 9-inch unbaked pie shell

Combine dry ingredients in an electric mixing bowl and mix well. Add eggs one at a time until each has mixed thoroughly. Add remaining wet ingredients in same manner. Pour mixture into a 9-inch unbaked pie shell and bake in a 350-degree oven for 30 to 45 minutes. Cool on rack. Top with brown sugar meringue. Yields 1 pie.

Topping

2 large egg whites at room
    temperature
⅓ teaspoon cream of tartar

½ cup brown sugar
1 teaspoon lemon juice

Cool electric mixer bowl and blades in a freezer, if possible. Whip egg whites and cream of tartar in mixer until foamy. Slowly add in lemon juice and brown sugar until stiff peaks form. Raise oven temperature to 400-degrees and spoon meringue on top of pie evenly. Bake for 5 to 10 minutes until pie is golden brown. Chill and serve. Serves 6.

Photo courtesy of Old Salem, Inc.

Old Salem Tavern

736 South Main Street

WINSTON-SALEM

No, George Washington never ate here. However, for two nights in 1791, he did lodge at the original Salem Tavern. He probably bypassed the "publick room" where the "ordinary" were served, eating instead in the "gentlemen's room." Just imagine the bearded Moravian brethren rubbing shoulders —or more probably, lifting a tankard of ale—with the Father of Our Country.

Today, as guests sit in Windsor chairs at tables set with pewter, the Tavern's wait staff in period costume offer the same "kindness and cordiality" as stipulated by the original Moravian elders. The Moravians, a devout sect founded in Eastern Europe in the fifteenth century, came to North Carolina by way of Georgia and Pennsylvania. The first settlers arrived here in 1753 and eventually built a planned community, keeping their strict code of morality intact. Records note that the brethren didn't frown on the use of spirits; it was the "deleterious influence of strangers" that caused them to limit the tavern, when they could, to "traveling strangers only." By the time of the Revolution, the tavern was famous throughout the Southeast for the "high quality of food and drink taken amid hospitable surroundings."

The tavern became so popular that, in 1815, a second building was erected next door to house the overflow. It is in this building that you may dine beside a traditional Moravian fireplace or under a candle sconce that makes a flickering, butterfly-shaped shadow on the foot-thick wall. In the warmer months the wisteria-cloaked arbor is always inviting, as is the wide selection of spirits that remains part of the Tavern's fare.

At dinner I am inclined toward Rack of Lamb dusted with Rosemary and Bread Crumbs. Duck is another favorite, as is Moravian Chicken Pie. Be sure to try the Pumpkin Muffins, too. For dessert I am torn between the outrageously rich Chocolate Amaretto Pie or traditional Moravian Gingerbread.

Be sure to set aside a day for touring the restored village of Old Salem, nestled near the towers of modern downtown Winston-Salem.

Lunch
11:30 A.M. to 2:00 P.M.
Sunday—Friday
(until 2:30 P.M. Sunday)

Dinner
5:30 P.M. to 9:00 P.M.
Monday—Thursday

5:30 P.M. to 9:30 P.M.
Friday and Saturday.

For reservations, call
(336) 748-8585.

www.oldsalem.org/visit/
dining.org

The cobbled streets and period architecture impart a sense of serenity. Salem, after all, derives from the Hebrew word for peace.

Old Salem Tavern's Moravian Chicken Pie

Filling and Sauce

1 whole large chicken	4 cups chicken stock
salt	splash of white wine
pepper	1 pint half-and-half
bay leaf	dashes of Tabasco &
½ cup butter	Worcestershire sauce
½ cup flour	egg wash (see recipe)

Boil chicken until meat is ready to fall off the bone. Let cool. Pick meat off and dice; set aside. Put all remaining chicken parts back in water; add seasonings (salt, pepper, bay leaf, etc.). Simmer for a few hours, strain.

Melt butter in a saucepan on medium heat and add flour. Stir until smooth; add stock and a splash of white wine. Cook and stir until thickened. Lower heat and add half-and-half and stir until smooth. Add Tabasco and Worcestershire sauce and mix. Add half of the sauce to chicken meat and fill the pie shell. Cover with second pie dough sheet. Crimp edges and cut slits in top to vent.

Mix 1 egg white with a tablespoon of water. Brush egg wash on top crust. Bake at 350 degrees until golden brown. Yields 1 pie.

Pie Dough (makes one 10-inch double-crust pie)

2½ cups flour	1 egg
¾ cup butter	3 tablespoons sour cream

Mix flour and butter and press until crumbly. Add the egg and sour cream, but keep coarse. Roll pie dough out in 2 sheets. Grease a 10-inch pie pan and line with 1 sheet. Reserve second sheet (see above).

Old Salem Tavern's Chocolate Amaretto Pie

Crust

1½ cups plain chocolate cookies, crumbled (Oreo® wafers may be used; remove filling first)	½ cup almond paste
	¼ cup butter, melted
	Non-stick cooking spray

Put cookies in a food processor and process until they are the consistency of crumbs. Add almond paste and butter and process until blended. Apply non-stick cooking spray to a 9½- or 10-inch, deep-dish pie pan. Spread mixture evenly. Bake in a preheated 400-degree oven for 5 minutes.

Filling

1 egg yolk	2 tablespoons rum
2 tablespoons almond paste	16 ounces semisweet chocolate
2 tablespoons instant coffee	¼ cup melted butter
1 cup whipping cream	2 egg whites
1 tablespoon brandy	2 tablespoons powdered sugar
2 tablespoons Amaretto liqueur	

In a food processor, add egg yolk, almond paste, coffee, 3 tablespoons of whipping cream, brandy, amaretto, and rum. Process until smooth. In a double boiler, melt chocolate over hot, not boiling, water. Add melted chocolate and butter to the mixture and process until blended. Let cool. In an electric mixer, beat egg whites with powdered sugar. Beat in remaining whipping cream. Fold into chocolate mixture gently. Pour into piecrust. Refrigerate 4 hours. Yields 1 pie.

Old Salem Tavern's Gingerbread

⅔ cup sugar	2 eggs
¾ cup butter, softened	rind of 1 orange, grated
⅓ cup honey	2 tablespoons grated ginger
⅓ cup molasses	2 teaspoons baking powder
⅔ cup milk	2 cups plain flour

Preheat oven to 350 degrees. Cream together sugar and butter in a bowl. Add honey and molasses. Mix until smooth. Add milk, eggs, and grated orange rind. Sift spices and baking powder with flour and add to batter. Mix until smooth. Place in a 12-by-9-inch greased and floured baking pan. Bake until browned, about 15 minutes. Turn heat down to 200 degrees and bake for 60 to 90 minutes or until a toothpick comes out clean.

Las Palmas Restaurant & Bar

122 East Fisher Street

SALISBURY

$\mathcal{W}$ ise preservationists often retain quirky little features of the past in a historic building. Such is the case at Las Palmas, which occupies a two-story building erected in 1903 as a warehouse for Wallace and Sons Dry Goods Store. To move notes between the ground floor and second story, twenty-two feet above, a small container zipped back and forth on a cable. High-tech then, it's good for a smile in the twenty-first century.

The building once was home to Friendly Q Billiards, known as the largest pool hall in North Carolina, and later it became a car dealership. In 1985, the building was added to the National Historic Register of Places.

Lunch
11:00 A.M. to 2:00 P.M.
Tuesday—Friday.

Dinner
5:00 P.M. to 9:30 P.M.
Sunday—Thursday.

Bar
Until 10:30 P.M.
Friday and Saturday.

Reservations not required.
(704) 636-9475.

Salisbury, one of North Carolina's most historic towns, in colonial times sat at the intersection of the North-South Trail (also known as the Presbyterian Trail) and the East-West Trail. President George Washington visited in 1791, noting that he much preferred the sophistication of Salisbury to Charlotte, "a trifling little town."

John Gray owns Las Palmas, which serves Mexican and Southwestern fare, and he once was the chef. Gray candidly admits he entered the restaurant business with no background in cooking. His first time in the kitchen, he says wryly, was his "first day on the job. Of course, I did improve."

The menu offers choices for those folks who haven't yet latched onto Tex-Mex. The selections include vegetarian dishes, oysters on the half-shell, peel-and-eat shrimp, and meatloaf with smoked Cheddar cheese.

Las Palmas serves a creamy Spinach Con Queso. Pickled jalapeños give this cheesy dish a tolerable kick. "Hot off the skillet" is taken literally here, where Steak & Chicken Fajitas arrive in the skillet, still cooking. The padded skillet handle is a thoughtful touch, making it easy to maneuver. These South Texas Fajitas feature marinated steak and chicken, grilled onions and peppers, Pico de Gallo, guacamole, sour cream, and beans inside a tortilla. (The Pico de Gallo carries quite a punch, so eat slowly.)

My Bunuelos dessert was a deep-fried tortilla sprinkled with a sugar-cinnamon mixture, drizzled with chocolate syrup and dressed with whipped cream. The Bunuelos tasted like Good Humor chocolate bars and reminded me of the ice cream truck I used to run after as a child.

People come to Las Palmas for more than just the food. Salisbury natives refer to Las Palmas as their "Cheers." There's occasional live entertainment, and Tuesday is Open Mike Night. Otherwise the music is jazz, R &B, and blues. This is a good-time place where you feel comfortable and well fed.

Las Palmas' Chicken Fajitas

Marinade

½ cup lime juice
½ tablespoon fresh jalapeño peppers, minced
½ cup red wine vinegar
½ tablespoon crushed red pepper
1 cup water
1½ teaspoons ground black pepper

¼ cup soy sauce
¼ cup onion, diced
½ tablespoon fresh garlic, chopped
¼ cup canola oil
2 to 3 pounds, boneless, skinless chicken breasts

Mix all ingredients except chicken. Place chicken in a large bowl or large, zippered plastic bag. Add marinade. Cover bowl or seal bag. Refrigerate over night.

Fajitas

6 to 8 flour or corn tortillas
½ cup, or more, sour cream
½ cup, or more, Pico de Gallo

2 medium onions, sliced
2 bell peppers, sliced

Remove the chicken from container and grill or broil about eight to ten minutes on each side, depending on thickness. Chicken is done when meat is no longer pink at thickest part when pierced with a tester or fork. Grill or broil onions and peppers. Combine onions, peppers, and chicken in flour or corn tortillas with sour cream and Pico de Gallo (recipe follows). Serves 6 to 8.

Las Palmas' Pico de Gallo

1½ cups fresh roma
  tomatoes, diced
2 tablespoons red wine vinegar
¾ cup diced onions
½ bunch fresh cilantro
2 tablespoons fresh jalapeño
  peppers, diced

2 tablespoons lime juice
¼ tablespoon ground black
  pepper
½ tablespoon olive oil
½ tablespoon salt
¼ tablespoon sugar

Mix all of the ingredients. Serve atop grilled or broiled chicken, or use with refried beans and guacamole. Yields over 2 cups.

Las Palmas' Spinach Con Queso

2½ pounds white American
  cheese, suitable for melting
6 cups whole milk
1½ cups jalapeño pepper
  juice from cans of jalapeños
¼ cup pickled jalapeños
¼ cup tomatoes, diced
1 teaspoon ground black
  pepper

½ tablespoon cumin
½ teaspoon fresh jalapeños,
  chopped
1 cup onions, diced
½ cup spinach, chopped
½ cup Anaheim chilies from
  can
corn chips

Put American cheese, milk, and jalapeño pepper juice in the top of a double boiler on simmering heat. Stir mixture as cheese begins to melt and continue stirring until smooth. Put mixture in a large saucepan and add all other ingredients except chips. Stir to combine and cook on medium to medium-low heat for about an hour. Stir frequently to keep from sticking. Remove and let cool. Serve in bowls with chips for dipping. Serves 6 to 8.

The McNinch House

511 North Church Street
CHARLOTTE

he first moment Ellen Davis saw Sam McNinch's Victorian-style home, she told a friend, "I'm going to buy that house." Some things one just feels deep in one's soul. Even after learning of its needed repairs, she never wavered from her goal—a *tres elegante* restaurant.

Dinner
6:30 P.M. until,
Tuesday—Saturday.

Reservations are a must:
(704) 332-6159.

At her restaurant, guests would be treated as valued friends. She would prepare dinners combining traditional Southern gentility with New South cuisine. Tables would be set with her collection of antique sterling silver, crystal, and china. She would entertain as Charlotte Mayor Sam McNinch did in 1909, when President William Howard Taft dined here after speaking at Charlotte's annual celebration of "Meck-Dec" Day.

Davis has accomplished every goal, and more, all without advertising. As manager Greg Hardee says, "There is no need to advertise. The person who needs us, finds us." Then he adds, "But you don't just pop in. You call for a reservation, and we mail you a list of six entrées to choose from. Ellen chooses the other five courses, and the four wines that she pairs with your six courses. Dinner takes three hours, so bring a friend."

I chose lobster from the list of entrées, and my friend Jane Brock selected salmon. On a December evening, dressed in our best, we drove up to the home built in 1891 at a cost of thirty-five thousand dollars. A valet met us at the driveway, and we were greeted by Hardee in the beautiful foyer. He led us back to the sitting room, where we talked about the home's history as our host passed crab appetizers and poured glasses of a melodic Spanish Cava Champagne.

At our table, ruby and white crystal sat beside ornate china and early eighteenth-century sterling that glistened in candlelight. Our Artichoke Soup tasted as beguiling and vivid as the African daisy in its center. The paired wine was a light and lilting Maconaise White Burgundy. Then an eye-candy Arugula Salad, wearing an edible purple orchid, appeared.

The next pairing was a palate-cleansing Passion-Fruit Sorbet in green martini glasses, served with a subtle Chardonnay. My entrée, Lobster Tail, sat upon a mound of rich, but not overwhelming, sauce—exquisite indulgence! A French Pinot Noir was a perfect complement, and the baby pink rose beside it set the ambiance.

Ellen Davis never studied cooking, so how can she cook like this? Her mother, she explains, didn't like to cook. So, from the time Ellen could stand on a Coca-Cola crate, she cooked. Pretty soon imagination led to experimenting. That's when she began trying novel ingredients for standard dishes, not unlike her method today. Lots of experiments do get pitched, but the successes are worth it, especially for something as superb as the Tomato-Vodka Sauce that cradled my lobster. Jane's Saucy Salmon rendered the same effect. Quality ingredients also play a role, Hardee explained. "Our salmon is flown in from Norway within a day of being caught," he said.

At McNinch's, details matter. Watch as the waiter places an heirloom linen doily on the saucer below your empty coffee cup. No clinking china should disturb this setting, nor should a cell phone. Naturally, men are required to wear jackets at all times.

Dessert—White Chocolate Mousse with rich Whipped Cream—was understated true love, and serving it with a large red rose didn't dim the romance. The rose lasted for a week; memories of the evening at this magic-making place will last much longer. On my first visit to McNinch's, Hardee had a twinkle in his eye as he said, "We care more about your experience than you do." A visit is all the convincing you'll need. A dining experience at McNinch's is the epitome of what it means to be Southern.

McNinch's Artichoke Soup

¼ cup unsalted butter
½ cup garlic, minced
4 cups yellow onions, chopped
½ tablespoon salt
1¾ pounds artichokes, chopped

½ tablespoon dried thyme
1 teaspoon mace
tiny pinch of cayenne pepper
8 cups whole milk
1 pint heavy cream
4 cups chicken broth

In a large soup pot set on medium-high, melt butter and add garlic and onions. Sauté until translucent and add salt, stirring to incorporate. Lower heat medium-low and stir in artichokes, thyme, mace, and cayenne, and cook for about 2 minutes. Add milk, cream and broth and cook on low for about 2 to 3 hours. Taste, and cook longer if needed, and adjust seasoning. Serves about 16.

Note: freezes beautifully in tight containers.

McNinch's Lobster Tail with Tomato-Vodka Sauce

Tomato-Vodka Sauce

2 tablespoons butter
2 cups yellow onions, chopped
1 tablespoon garlic, minced
1 teaspoon salt

4 medium tomatoes, peeled,
*   deseeded, chopped*
½ cup vodka
1 pint heavy cream

Melt butter on medium-high in a skillet; sauté onions and garlic until golden. Stir in salt. Add tomatoes and vodka and cook until
very thick. Pour cream into a saucepan and reduce on medium heat
to a sauce consistency. Watch carefully in order not to burn.

Lobster Tail

4 7-ounce lobster tails
2 tablespoons butter

Tomato-Vodka Sauce (above)

Remove lobster meat from shells and cut to bite-size pieces. Sauté
in butter until done. Drain excess liquid. Add Tomato-Vodka Sauce.
Serve over favorite cooked pasta. McNinch House uses Cheese Ravioli. Serves 4.

McNinch's White Chocolate Mousse with Whipped Cream

½ pound white chocolate
¾ cup macadamia nuts,
*   chopped*

1 cup heavy whipping cream
Raspberry Sauce (optional)

Melt chocolate in a double boiler and stir in the nuts. Whip cream
until stiff peaks form; fold whipped cream carefully into chocolate
mixture. Divide mixture equally between 4 wine glasses. Garnish
with prepared raspberry sauce and serve. Serves 4.

Pewter Rose Bistro

1820 South Boulevard
CHARLOTTE

he Pewter Rose is the definition of fun. That, and the food, are why I've climbed the outside staircase to the second floor of this 1925 building time and again. It's a come-as-you-are restaurant, which is unusual for an upper-end establishment, but it works. The trendsetting owner, Susie Smith-Peck, has a knack for serendipitous décor, which continually evolves.

She initially favored an eclectic, thirties-style design that featured old lace with pink tablecloths. The current look includes more than sixty colorful glass vases illuminated with tiny white lights. The collection sits atop two walls of a private dining room; beneath them the room resembles a den with bookshelves, but look closer. Each book bears the

Lunch
11:00 A.M. to 2:00 P.M.
Monday—Saturday.

Sunday Brunch
10:00 A.M. to 3:00 P.M.

Dinner
5:00 P.M. to 10:00 P.M.
Monday—Thursday.
11:00 P.M. Friday, Saturday.
9:00 P.M. Sunday.

Reservations are needed
for parties over 6.
Call (704) 332-8149.

name of a wait-person. Outside this room, several star-shaped paper lamps hang from the wood-beamed ceiling. Lots of greenery contrasts with the warmth of the red-brick walls. With each visit you'll see something different, which is why Pewter Rose Bistro is fun.

You have to wonder what the original owners of this mill building would say if they saw folks sitting on sofas and easy chairs in the bistro's bar. Or went to the ladies' room and found walls painted to resemble artist Claude Monet's lilies in the pond. Textile mill workers once put in long hours here; nowadays, chef Blake Dewey and pastry chef Kyle Burke do likewise.

Smith-Peck describes their food as international ethnic cuisine. I understood what she meant when I tasted my appetizer of Lobster and Crab Daikon Rolls, served on a blue-and-gray oriental plate. (If you've not previously bought daikon, a type of radish, now you have good reason to try it.) Dip lobster-filled daikon into a spicy-nice rosemary juice mixed with ginger. The tongue tingles with Thai flavors. That was followed by an entrée of Sweet and Spicy Lamb Brochettes. The brown sugar and curry marinade is almost Tex-Mex hot, but fresh pineapple cools and enhances the lamb's unique flavor.

The bistro uses flavorful and juicy free-range chicken for its entrée of Indonesian Chicken. Coconut milk marinated with lemon grass delivers an authentic Asian taste. All of the bistro's herbs are locally grown. This ensures their freshness and helps support a network of community growers.

The bistro's organically grown coffee is rich and dessert-like. Dewey noted that the high-quality beans come from shade-grown plants, a more natural and environmentally friendly method of cultivation. I had a tall cup with samples of Burke's Orange Grand Marnier Cake and his moist Apple and Spice Cake. You can't go wrong with either. The next time I come for dinner, I'll make sure that my visit is on Wednesday, Friday, or Saturday when there's live jazz.

Pewter Rose's Indonesian Chicken

½ stalk lemon grass
½ tablespoon curry powder
¼ cup cilantro
½ teaspoon fresh black pepper
1½ shallots, chopped
1/8 teaspoon kosher salt
2 garlic cloves, minced

1 tablespoon quality fish sauce
½ inch ginger, minced
1 tablespoon brown sugar
½ cup coconut milk
4 6-ounce chicken breasts, with skin

In a food processor or heavy blender purée all ingredients, one at a time, except for coconut milk and chicken breasts. Pour milk in last and blend well to incorporate. Pour marinade in a bowl large enough to accommodate and cover the chicken. Cover bowl and refrigerate for 1 to 2 days, turning occasionally. Slice and grill chicken on all sides until golden brown. Serves 4.

Pewter Rose's Sweet and Spicy Lamb Marinade

¼ medium yellow onion, minced
2 tablespoons garlic, minced
¾ teaspoon kosher salt
2 tablespoons cider vinegar
1 tablespoon brown sugar
1 tablespoon curry powder
¾ teaspoon turmeric

¾ teaspoon black pepper, fresh
¾ teaspoon cayenne pepper
2 tablespoons lemon juice, fresh
1 bay leaf
½ cup extra virgin olive oil
2 pounds top round lamb

For Skewers

½ green bell pepper, cut into 2-inch squares
8 1½-inch pieces of pineapple

½ red bell pepper, cut into 2-inch squares

Purée all marinade ingredients, pouring oil last in a slow stream. Slice lamb in 1½- to 2-inch slices and put in a large bowl. Pour marinade over lamb pieces, cover and refrigerate for 1 to 2 days. Remove lamb from marinade. Alternate lamb, peppers, and pineapple when threading on skewers. Grill until lamb is done. Serve with Mango Chutney. Serves 4.

Pewter Rose's Mango Chutney

1 cup fresh pineapple, small diced
1½ cups fresh mango, peeled and diced
1½ tablespoons fresh mint, minced

1½ tablespoons fresh lime juice
½ teaspoon kosher salt
2 tablespoons red onion, diced
1 tablespoon red bell pepper, diced

Blend all ingredients together in a food processor or blender. Cover and refrigerate. (Can be made 1 day before the lamb.) To serve, fan out chutney on plate and center lamb.

River House Country Inn & Restaurant

1896 Old Field Creek Road
GRASSY CREEK

hefs spend their lives creating. Their skills employ science and art, which chef Bill Klein says, "gives them the ability to control and manipulate flavor." To these chefs cooking is not just a job, it's a calling. That's why, for years now, I've driven out of my way to Gayle Winston's River House.

Comfort and atmosphere enhance the dining experience. At River House, I like to sit in a rocking chair on Dr. Uriah Ballou's 1870 front porch and watch the day disappear over the New River. This is my ideal place to sip a glass of wine and unwind. The stone and timber home features a sophisticated, yet not imposing, dining room. It is graced with a few contemporary paintings, an old fireplace, and a grand piano that is often played.

Dinner
Wednesday — Sunday
Two seatings:
6:00 P.M. and 8:00 P.M.

For reservations
for the inn or dinner,
call (336) 982-2109.

www.riverhousenc.com

For my entrée I chose Chef Klein's Cornish Game Hen with Risotto and a Haricot Vert Salad. I've eaten many good Cornish Game Hen recipes, but Chef Klein's is the first that took two days to prepare. Klein, trained in France, kindly supplied for us a version of his recipe that can be prepared a bit more quickly. I also sampled the Pork Loin Risotto. As expected, it was juicy and sauced to perfection.

The fresh salad of Haricot Vert (green string beans) was good, too. When I eat River House vegetables, I remember the time the proprietor broke her foot and was unable to cook dinner. Amy, the manager, had to pinch-hit. Amy cooks well, but had to repeatedly run upstairs with samples of glazes before Winston, who was sitting up in bed peeling carrots, gave them her approval. Perhaps that attention to detail is why everything tastes so perfect here.

Coffee came next, to settle the many flavors before dessert. A healthy fresh fruit tart seemed my likely choice, but it was overruled by Winston's luxuriously rich Chocolate-Kahlúa Truffles with Ground Espresso. Good simply fails to describe these truffles; opulent is more accurate.

Braising Liquid

1 yellow onion, diced
1 leek, white only, diced
1 large carrot, diced
2 tablespoons Canola oil
2 bay leaves

2 star anise, or fennel seeds
1 teaspoon black peppercorns
3 sprigs thyme
3 sprigs parsley
2 garlic cloves, crushed

In a large oven-safe pot, cook vegetables in oil over medium heat until onions are translucent. Meanwhile, make a sachet from cheesecloth. Put herbs inside and tie with twine to create a mirepoix sachet.

Game Hens

2 cups chicken stock
salt and pepper to taste
1 mirepoix sachet
4 vine ripe tomatoes, diced

2 tablespoons butter
1 tablespoon oil
2 Cornish game hens
risotto rice for 4

Add homemade or prepared chicken stock, sachet, and tomatoes to braising liquid and simmer. Cut away hen's legs; salt and pepper legs and put in a sauté pan in hot oil. Sear until browned on both sides. Add legs to braising liquid. Cover with a tight-fitting lid and put in a 350-degree oven for 45 to 60 minutes. Done when thigh-bone is easily removed. Cool, uncovered, in braising liquid.

Prepare risotto rice for 4 according to package instructions.

Season hen breasts on both sides with salt and pepper. Add a tablespoon of Canola oil to another sauté pan and heat until smoking. Add breasts skin-side down. Brown evenly. Turn breasts and brown other side. Add butter and a large sprig of thyme to pan. Tilt pan to spoon butter over breasts to baste. Breasts are done when the tip of a pairing knife, inserted into center of a breast for 5 to 10 seconds, comes out warm and all juices run clear. Ladle Braising Liquid onto warmed plates; add a mound of risotto to each. Place a leg and a breast (whole or half) over risotto. Serves 2 to 4.

River House's Chocolate-Kahlúa Espresso Truffles

12-ounces bittersweet or
semi-sweet chocolate
½ cup unsalted butter
1 teaspoon vanilla extract
1 tablespoon Kahlúa liqueur

4 egg yolks
½ cup sugar
⅓ cup espresso beans,
ground fine

In the top of a double-boiler melt chocolate and butter over simmering heat, stirring until combined. Remove immediately. Add vanilla and Kahlúa. Gradually whisk into 4 lightly beaten egg yolks until thoroughly mixed. Cool, cover, and chill without stirring. Combine sugar with ground espresso beans and scatter on a large piece of wax paper. Use a small melon baller or round measuring teaspoon to scoop out truffle pieces. Roll each scoopful into a ball and roll over sugar mixture to cover all sides. Set each covered truffle on another clean sheet of wax paper until finished. Keep cool. Yields about 30 to 35 truffles.

Shatley Springs Inn

407 Shatley Springs Road / N.C. 16
CRUMPLER

*M*aybe the food at Shatley Springs Inn is the major drawing card today, but that was not always the case. The inn began in the early 1900s as a health resort.

Open Daily
7:00 A.M. to 9:00 P.M.
May—October.

For reservations
call (336) 982-2236.

www.shatleysprings.com

Martin Shatley claimed that for over seven years he was so ill with consumption and other painful diseases that doctors pronounced him incurable. Believing that he was near death, Shatley bought a farm in 1890 to provide for his family's welfare. Soon after, Shatley passed a spring on his land and stopped to bathe his inflamed face. He declared that in less than an hour the healing process had begun. After only a few days of bathing in the spring water his fever disappeared, and in three weeks, he was well enough to do heavy farm labor. His statement further asserts that in the ensuing thirty-five years he witnessed the cure of people with skin diseases, rheumatism, and nervous disorders.

I was curious to see the spring providing these curative waters, which according to analysts is especially high in calcium, magnesium, and five other healthful minerals. But the aroma of fried chicken drew me into the main dining room.

Over twenty years ago I overheard a man say, "I bet you could have a good meal by eating the crumbs off this table." I could easily have heard a similar remark when I stopped by last summer. The tables are still crammed with dishes served "family style." This is an inn that offers properly seasoned country food. From Coleslaw to Strawberry Cobbler, the flavor is there. Diners can choose entrées such as Chicken Pie or Fried Chicken. The cook laughed when I asked for the Fried Chicken recipe, a well-kept secret. On my last visit my waitress told me that her mother had worked at Shatley for years and still didn't know the Fried Chicken recipe.

The fabulous vegetables are cooked with half-and-half, real butter, and a little flour. What a difference the real thing makes. This is not the type of place you would think of for a dieter, but they continue to serve cottage cheese with fresh fruit dishes.

A few things have changed. The inn no longer cures its country hams, but you can buy one at their country store from a supplier. The store is new, and the dining rooms have been redecorated in a smart, but still comfortable look. You'll usually find country, bluegrass, and gospel entertainment on Saturday nights. Alcoholic beverages are neither served nor allowed, and that philosophy seems to be in harmony with the healing minerals of the spring outside. But you don't see people lining up at the spring to fill empty milk jugs as I once saw.

It is reassuring to find that some very good places have not changed significantly.

Shatley Springs Inn's Coleslaw

1 head cabbage
1/4 cup onion, diced
1/2 cup milk
1/4 cup sugar

1/2 cup mayonnaise
2 tablespoons vinegar
1/2 teaspoon salt
1/2 teaspoon pepper

Shred cabbage. Place all ingredients in a medium-size mixing bowl and stir to combine. Correct seasoning to taste. Cover and refrigerate. Serves 4.

Shatley Springs Inn's Creamed Potatoes

8 potatoes, peeled and
   quartered
1 teaspoon salt

1/4 cup butter
1 tablespoon or more flour
2 cups half-and-half

In a medium pot, place potatoes, salt, and water to cover. Boil until potatoes are tender; drain. Add butter, flour, and half-and-half. Mix with an electric mixer until smooth and thick. Serve hot. Serves 6 to 8.

Shatley Springs Inn's Strawberry Cobbler

2 cups strawberries, lightly
   chopped
pinch of salt
1 cup sugar
½ teaspoon cinnamon
¼ teaspoon nutmeg
1 teaspoon lemon juice

2 tablespoons butter
1 handful (¼ cup) fresh
   strawberries, cut up
1 unbaked pie crust
   (homemade or commercial)
brown sugar

Mix strawberries, salt, sugar, cinnamon, nutmeg, and lemon juice and put into a greased, oven-safe, shallow 8- to 9-inch baking dish. Dot with butter and sprinkle with rest of strawberries. Roll out pie crust and cover bowl. Sprinkle top of crust with brown sugar. Bake at 350 degrees for about 40 minutes. Yields 1 cobbler.

The Best Cellar Restaurant

Off U.S. 321 By-Pass at 267 Little Springs Road
BLOWING ROCK

The Best Cellar Restaurant owes its existence to a lucky flip of a coin. Had the coin landed the other way, founder Ira Wilson would have made toys in a Christian commune in Pennsylvania. Instead, he brought his family and his "food for the heart" south.

The Best Cellar began in a basement in downtown Blowing Rock, near a Christian bookstore operated by Ira's wife, Lani. Locals helped the restaurant succeed, pitching in with favorite recipes and managerial ideas. The formula worked. The restaurant outgrew its downtown location, leading the family to convert their log-cabin home, built in 1938, into one of this mountain resort's most sought-after restaurants. When I discovered it, getting a reservation took three tries.

The restaurant now is operated by Rob Dyer and Lisa Stripling. The wise new owners have not changed a thing, including favorite recipes. The bar, formerly a guesthouse, still has its rustic look with three fireplaces and beamed ceiling. Stained-glass doves still flank the handsome arched door that leads into the dining room.

Our party filled two tables in front of a fireplace decorated with live sunflowers. Peach-colored Fiesta ware, wooden candlesticks, and new wineglasses were arranged on a fresh, old-fashioned-style tablecloth. One friend, a wine aficionado, was thrilled to find her favorite California and international wines available.

I was more thrilled that Stuffed Zucchini, a dish I often serve at dinner parties, was on the menu. Vegetables are an afterthought in some restaurants, but not at the Best Cellar. Parsley Potatoes, Rice, and to-die-for Home-Baked Breads were just like my grandmother made.

Plenty of modern treatments complement the old-fashioned vegetables and décor, and presentation continues to reign high, with each dish looking as if ready for a food magazine photo shoot. That includes the salad, served with a special warm Shallot and Smoked Bacon Vinaigrette or creamy Vinaigrette Dijon.

Our group did a lot of bite sharing. I ordered Shrimp Provençal, a favorite at the Best Cellar. Sherry sauce complements the robust-tasting shrimp. One friend had the Veal Scaloppini a la Crème, whose delicate, creamy sauce doesn't overpower the mild veal. Another went for the house specialty, Fresh Yellowfin Tuna Marinade. Excellent olive oil combines with soy, fresh herbs, and ginger, which gives this dish a bounce!

The *piece de résistance* is Banana Cream Pie, a rich and creamy wonder that embodies the restaurant's philosophy—superb ingredients imaginatively woven into a soul- and appetite-nurturing experience.

The Best Cellar's Stuffed Zucchini

3 medium zucchini, whole
1 cup medium-sharp Cheddar cheese, grated
2 ounces cream cheese, softened
3 tablespoons butter
2 cups Spanish onions, chopped
¼ to ⅓ cup pecans, chopped

2 heaping tablespoons dill
2 heaping tablespoons sweet basil
⅓ cup whole-wheat bread crumbs
3 to 4 slices Swiss cheese, cut in 1-inch strips
paprika to taste

Parboil zucchini. Cool and slice in half lengthwise. Scoop pulp from zucchini and strain through cheesecloth. Reserve ½ cup of pulp (discard remainder or save for other use). Set aside zucchini shells. Mix grated Cheddar cheese and softened cream cheese in a medium-size bowl. In skillet, heat butter and sauté onions until very brown. Mix in pecans, dill, sweet basil, and ½ cup zucchini pulp. Add breadcrumbs, mixing thoroughly. Add skillet contents to cheeses and mix thoroughly. Stuff 6 reserved zucchini shells with mixture and top with Swiss cheese strips. Bake in a preheated 400-degree oven for 15 to 20 minutes. Sprinkle paprika on top. Serves 6.

The Best Cellar's Shrimp Provençal

8 tablespoons butter, divided
½ cup dry sherry
3 large garlic cloves, minced
1 cup Spanish onions,
    chopped
1 pound shrimp, deveined
    with tails left intact

3 medium tomatoes, skinned,
    seeded and chopped
½ cup fresh basil or ½ tea-
    spoon dried basil
salt to taste
white pepper to taste
1 cup scallions, chopped

Place 4 tablespoons of chilled butter in a cold skillet with sherry. Blend as heat is slowly raised to medium-high, being very careful not to let sauce break down. Add onion and garlic and sauté until almost tender. Add shrimp, tomatoes, and basil and sauté until shrimp just begin to turn pink. Add salt and pepper. Add remaining 4 tablespoons of butter and stir in scallions, sautéing until shrimp is done. Place mixture on warm plates, with rice on the side. Serves 4.

Crippen's Restaurant

239 Sunset Drive

BLOWING ROCK

The first episode of *Taste of Adventure*, based on my historic restaurant books, was filmed nearly 20 years ago for UNC-TV. Our film crew ran the Nolichucky River, where we met a memorable daredevil of a young man. No one imagined then that he would become an owner of one of Blowing Rock's most fantastic restaurants.

Over the years our family often has celebrated at Crippen's, where the food is consistently superb. But I never realized until a recent visit that the daredevil I met on the river is the same Jimmy Crippen, restaurateur. His metamorphosis is a love story, which he explained over dinner in the classic/rustic ambiance of his restaurant.

Years ago Jimmy fell in love with a girl from Florida named Carolyn. He followed her there, taking a job as a restaurant busboy. Within a year he became the manager, working with chef James Welch, another North Carolinian. Jimmy and Carolyn married and eventually returned to Blowing Rock, along with their chef friend.

The restaurant trio considered several possibilities before purchasing the 1931 Sunshine Inn boardinghouse. That was in 1994, and they spent a year remodeling it into a spiffy bed-and-breakfast. Carolyn designed a French-country dining room, separate bar, and chef's kitchen. While planting herbs in her back yard, she found a slew of broken dishes. Research revealed boardinghouse waiters and kitchen help hid broken dishes out back. If guilt was admitted, the breaker was charged. Hence, the burial.

Jimmy started me off with a Portobello and Sweet Vermouth Soup. These so-called fusion dishes can sound outlandish, but this creamy soup is unique and tasty.

Crippen's has brought the exotic to Blowing Rock, such as Kangaroo cooked in Coca-Cola. When Welch adds chili, his kangaroo becomes a tender, tasty cousin of venison. With mashed potatoes and black-eyed peas on top, it's perfection.

Welch is one of those genius chefs who imagines new flavors, then assembles ingredients to make a dish work. Grilled Escarole Salad, accompanied with Beans, is a terrific example. Another is Steak In-fused with Chocolate, an odd-sounding combination for sure. But it tastes incredible! Crippen's will not divulge this recipe to anyone. "We told *Bon Appetit* no," Jimmy said.

This much we know: Welch rolls the steak in finely ground Turkish cookies, slits the steak sideways and stuffs it with bittersweet choco-late. It's the best steak you've ever had! One more thing: When the five breads are offered, try a different one each time.

I also sampled the Salmon with Japanese sauce, which spices but doesn't deplete salmon's innate personality. This healthful recipe tastes good enough for Sunday company. (In the South, that means serving your best.)

Welch's desserts also stand out. Even the sorbets have more body than usual, particularly the Passion Fruit Sorbet. The slightly peachy tone gains depth when Welch adds his secret syrup. The Vanilla Crème Brûlée is irresistible, and Welch's Apple Tart with homemade Cinna-mon Ice Cream, drizzled with Caramel Sauce, is pure comfort food.

Bon appetit for your dinner at Crippen's.

Crippen's Horseradish-Crusted Salmon

6 7-ounce cuts of salmon	2 tablespoons sour cream
salt	2 tablespoons wasabi
6 tablespoons horseradish	½ cup Mirin wine (Japanese)
1 cup breadcrumbs	½ ounce soy sauce
2 tablespoons butter	4 tablespoons sugar
5 medium potatoes, peeled, cooked	¼ cup heavy cream
	½ to 1 cup butter
6 tablespoons butter, melted	12 shallots, peeled and sliced

Salt the salmon. Combine horseradish and breadcrumbs and coat salmon. Melt 2 tablespoons butter and sear salmon on both sides in hot skillet; place in 375-degree oven for 5 to 8 minutes. Mash potatoes and add melted butter, sour cream, wasabi, 2 tablespoons of sugar, and sprinkling of salt. Place in skillet with salmon. Reduce Mirin, soy sauce, and 2 tablespoons of sugar, stirring until syrup-like; add cream and reduce until thick and bubbling. Slowly add chunks of butter, stirring until melted and incorporated. Season with salt. Fry shallots until crispy. Serve salmon with potatoes and gar-nish with shallots. Serves 6.

1 or 2 18-by-26-inch puff
    pastry sheets
1 jumbo-size egg white
1 tablespoon water
6 tablespoons almond
    paste

3 Granny Smith apples
6 teaspoons sugar
6 teaspoons cinnamon
6 teaspoons butter

Cut pastry into 6 squares. Be sure each is large enough to accommodate a tablespoon of almond paste in the center and half of a cored and sliced apple. (Pastry may need to be rolled out more to give extra room.) Mix egg white with water and stir until well blended. With a pastry brush apply mixture to the six cut pastry sheets. Put 1 tablespoon of almond in the center of each. Peel and core apples; slice very thin crossways. Surround almond paste with sliced apples. Mix sugar and cinnamon together. Sprinkle equal amounts on each tart. Place a teaspoon of butter on each tart and bake in a 350-degree oven for 7 minutes. Rotate the pan and bake for 7 minutes more. Serves 6.

Caramel Sauce

2 cups sugar
1 lemon, juiced
2 cups water

2 tablespoons butter
1 quart heavy cream

In a medium-size heavy saucepan put in sugar, water, juice of lemon, and butter on medium-high temperature. Stir frequently until mixture turns a brown color. Turn heat to low and slowly add cream. *Do not let boil!* Remove from burner immediately, until burner cools down. Set aside.

Serve with:
1 quart good quality vanilla
    ice cream

cinnamon to taste

Scoop out sufficient ice cream for 6 small servings and whip in cinnamon just to taste. To serve, place tart on a dessert plate, drizzle with warm caramel sauce and place desired amount of cinnamon ice cream on the side of tart. Serves 6.

The Mast Farm Inn
and Restaurant

2543 Broadstone Road
VALLE CRUCIS

$\mathcal{J}$oseph Mast, of Swedish descent, was born in 1764 in Randolph County. Yearning for a place of his own Mast traded his rifle and dog for a thousand-acre tract of land in the secluded, rolling hills of Valle Crucis. Mast built his home, a two-room cabin, around 1810. It remains today as the oldest inhabitable log cabin in Watauga County.

In 1885 Joseph's grandson Finley Mast built the current farmhouse. Originally the home had six rooms with a detached kitchen. The Masts began offering meals and rooms to tourists, enlarging the home in 1915 to thirteen bedrooms. It was called The Mast Farm, or simply Aunt Josie's and Uncle Finley's.

Besides running the house and managing a vegetable garden and dairy, Aunt Josie became a master weaver. She turned the original log cabin into a loom house and became famous for her coverlets, rugs and handbags. Some of her coverlets are in the collection of the Smithsonian.

Old-timers remember carloads of folks coming down on Sunday to stand around the springhouse and drink Aunt Josie's buttermilk. Author Elizabeth Gray Vining recalls in her book *Quiet Pilgrimage*, "Every day there appeared on the long, white-clothed table at which we all sat, fried chicken, ham, homemade sausage, hot biscuits and spoon bread, home-churned butter. . . . Once I counted twenty different dishes."

The Mast Farm Inn has been listed in the National Register of Historic Places since 1972 as "one of the most complete and best preserved groups of nineteenth-century farm buildings in Western North Carolina."

The home changed hands in 1984 when the Pressly family bought it. They rehabilitated it to inn status, with bathrooms, breakfasts, and Sunday dinners. In 1996 sisters Wanda Hinshaw-Schoenfeldt and Kay Hinshaw Philipp started a partnership to run the Mast Farm Inn. Coincidentally, another set of sisters, Josie Mast and her sister, Leona, had worked together at the inn much earlier.

The menu has undergone a major transformation with its cur-

Breakfast
Inn guests only.

Dinner
5:30 P.M. TO 9:00 P.M.
Thursday — Tuesday,
May 10 — October.

Thursday — Saturday
in winter.
Schedule varies.

For reservations
call (888) 963-5857.

www.mastfarminn.com

rent owners. The cuisine leans more toward continental techniques that use regional fresh foods, along with a few imports to add interest. I sampled a Cured Raw Carpaccio of Beef Tenderloin. Good beef is available in America, but truffle oil comes from France. I couldn't imagine actually eating raw meat, but since it was cured I gave it a try. The first bite was not a flavor that I recognized. The next bite let me know that truffle oil accents beef in a way that neither Tabasco nor grocery store steak sauce ever could.

For my second course I ordered the Blind Joe Salad purely because of its intriguing title. It turned out to be an exotic choice: fresh greens with kalamata olives, tomatoes concasse, colorful fried vegetable ribbons, and a lemon-feta oregano dressing that unlocked each ingredient.

Selecting an entrée was difficult because this is not a fried chicken kind of place. I chose the healthy Yellowfin Tuna topped with candied fennel wrapped in crispy eggplant and served on tomato concasse with tomato coulis, basil oil, and Sauce Choron.

I couldn't even think about dessert, and for me that's going some.

The grounds of the inn are lovely. I'm not sure I would trade my dog for the land, but I'm not sorry that Joseph Mast did.

Mast Farm Inn's Horseradish Sauce

⅓ cup cream sherry
½ cup heavy cream

¼ teaspoon prepared
horseradish
salt and pepper to taste

Reduce sherry by one-half in a small pan over medium heat. Add cream, horseradish, and salt and pepper. Heat to simmer and cook for about 5 minutes, stirring. Serve hot; drizzle on warm plate beneath Crab Cheesecake.

Crust

2 cups fresh bread crumbs
½ cup walnuts, chopped
½ cup butter, melted

½ cup Swiss cheese, grated
1 tablespoon parsley, minced

Preheat oven to 350 degrees. Combine bread crumbs, walnuts, butter, cheese, and parsley. Process in a food processor until the mixture resembles crumbs. Press into the bottom of a 10-inch springform pan.

Batter

1¾ pounds cream cheese
1 medium onion, diced
2 cups Swiss cheese,
    grated
⅓ cup heavy cream

1 tablespoon paprika
salt and pepper to taste
4 eggs
1 pound jumbo lump crabmeat

In an electric mixer cream the cream cheese with the onion, Swiss cheese, cream, paprika, and salt and pepper. Beat in the eggs one at a time, allowing each to mix thoroughly with other ingredients. Fold in the crabmeat carefully and pour into the springform pan. Bake at 350 for 45 minutes or until set. Cool; cut into wedges to serve. Yields 14 to 16 servings as an appetizer.

Morel's Restaurant

1 Banner Street

BANNER ELK

$\mathcal{F}$lavor can be what you make it. The best chefs learn this at good cooking schools or by apprenticing with master chefs. Technique is extremely important, but to become a great chef you need imagination. And that is what chef Dean Mitchell, owner of Morel's, has.

You'll find his French bistro tucked into the quaint mountain town of Banner Elk. This Floridian, who was born into the business, began cooking under his dad when he was a teenager. He then worked throughout Europe, principally France, learning what he needed from the masters. At the age of twenty-two he became chef of Café L' Europe in Palm Beach, staying for nine years. *Food and Wine* named him as one of the sixty best chefs in the nation.

Dinner
6:00 P.M. TO 9:00 P.M.
Tuesday — Sunday
April — October.

For reservations
call (828) 898-6866.

Over fourteen years ago Chef Mitchell brought his family to North Carolina for a vacation and decided that this was where he wanted to raise his children. He found an abandoned 1942 brick building that had once housed a shoe store, a donut shop, and a clothing store. It took four months to add a kitchen, bar, and dining room. Crystal chandeliers now hang above dark green banquettes offset with pine panels and mirrors.

This modest chef calls his food World Cuisine because he employs Asian, French, and Italian dishes as well as American. As you might guess, he puts morels in every dish that suits. They grow wild under North Carolina's apple trees, and he and his children, Eric and Kristen, pick them each year about mid-May.

When I saw my Honey and Tamari Seared Salmon with cashews on wild rice, I was reminded that inspired presentation can set your senses in motion. I scooped up salmon, nuts, and rice in each bite, closing my eyes and thinking about how each taste enhances the whole.

My Asparagus Salad was equally unique. Perfection is a saucy bit of ham with asparagus that has been lightly blanched and grilled with a stewed fig over baby spinach dressed with a sun-dried tomato sauce.

Mitchell's pastry chef makes her own peach, coffee, and vanilla ice cream, serving it with pound cake or a brownie. Toppings include fruit coulee or maple syrup. I can't imagine tasting a better peach ice cream: creamy, yet tart and sweet.

Morel's Asparagus and Prosciutto Salad with Fig and Sun-Dried Tomato Dressing

1 bunch of green or white
asparagus
8 cloves garlic, minced
4 fresh figs
½ cup salad oil
½ cup red wine vinegar
1 tablespoon sugar

salt and pepper to taste
6 ounces of arugula
6 ounces thin-sliced
prosciutto, cooked
3 ounces sun-dried tomatoes
chopped parsley, optional

Peel and blanche asparagus, poaching lightly. Chill asparagus. Roast garlic a few minutes. Sauté figs in a small saucepan on medium-high heat with a tablespoon of oil. Purée garlic and figs and set aside this dressing. Add remaining oil to the pan and stir in wine vinegar until well combined. Add sugar, salt, and pepper. Stir well. Cool to room temperature. To prepare, place arugula evenly in 4 to 6 salad plates. Place a small slice of prosciutto atop each plate and alternate with several asparagus spears. Add fig-and-garlic dressing and garnish with finely chopped tomatoes and parsley. Serves 4 to 6.

Morel's Honey- and Tamari-Seared Salmon on Cashew Wild Rice

2 cups wild rice
1 cup cashews, chopped
½ cup of tamari
½ cup honey, plus ¼ cup
2½ pounds of fresh salmon

juice of 1 lemon
salt and pepper to taste
2 leeks, julliened and fried
1 large tomato, chopped

151

Cook rice according to directions until just soft. Add cashews; stir and set aside to keep warm. In large sauté pan, set at low heat, pour in tamari and ½ cup of honey. Stir to thoroughly incorporate and cook until it thickens. Place salmon, skin side up, in same saucepan and cook, turning when needed, until it is coated and becomes dark brown. (Take care not to burn.)

For sauce use a small bowl. Mix lemon juice with ¼ cup of honey. Add salt and pepper to taste and stir until well combined. To serve, evenly place cashew rice in the center of 6 warm plates. Top with salmon. Add sauce, leeks, and garnish with chopped tomato. Serves 6.

Eseeola Lodge
at Linville Golf Club

175 Linville Avenue
LINVILLE

arvard Professor William James, who stayed in one of the first Linville Company inns in 1891, described the area as "one of the most poetic places I have ever been in . . . hills covered with primeval forests . . . filled with rhododendron, laurels, and azaleas that are ablaze with glory." The inn's gabled roof and wrap-around verandah were part of the charm then, and the architecture continues to charm visitors today.

The Cherokee, first inhabitants of these hills, called the area *Eseeola*, or "land of cliffs and rivers."

In 1926 the Linville Company built its "new" inn. The design held onto rusticity, but placed heavy emphasis on sophistication. Though updated many times since, the inn still offers close-to-nature comfort, where guests relax on deep-seating leather sofas and chairs. A huge stone fireplace and beamed ceiling complete the environment. Be sure to look at the cabinets filled with rare Majolica china. The atmosphere, where my friend Linda High and I enjoyed a cocktail, is perfect for taking the edge off a hectic day.

Our table looked out upon a rolling lawn accented with bright flowers. The view reminded us of a more gracious time and set the scene for haute cuisine. Every course presentation was picture-perfect, starting with Low Country Shrimp and Smoked Tomato. The spicy-sour sauce went quite well with the remoulade and awakened every taste bud. The Pork Loin that followed, glazed with Sorghum and Cinnamon, was exquisitely tender. The accompanying Butterbean Vinaigrette of Bacon, Corn, and Sweet Pepper made this one very chic Southern dish.

The meal offered so many unusual flavors that I chose a palate cleanser for dessert. The tangy taste of Lemon Sorbet was an excellent finale.

Three meals served daily from mid-May to mid-October (dates vary).

Dinner
5:30 P.M. TO 9:30 P.M.

For dinner or inn reservations call (800) 742-6717 or (828) 733-4311.

www.eseeolalodge.com

Eseeola's Chili-Glazed Porkchop with Apple Cider Pistachio Butter

2 Ancho chilies
3 cups orange juice, fresh
2 tablespoons fresh ginger,
    minced
juice of 1 lime
⅓ cup sugar
2 tablespoons sherry vinegar
2 tablespoons garlic, minced
3 tablespoons orange zest

2 teaspoons sherry vinegar
2 tablespoons coriander
1 tablespoon cardamom
2 teaspoons cinnamon
1 tablespoon kosher salt
2 chipotle in Adobo Sauce, minced
1½ tablespoons olive oil
4 1-inch-thick, bone-in porkchops

Reconstitute Ancho chilies in boiling water; remove and cool; remove seeds and mince chilies. Whisk together all ingredients except chipotle, oil, and porkchops in medium saucepan. Bring to a boil. Lower heat and simmer for 7 minutes, then remove from heat. Whisk in chipotle and olive oil and continue to whisk until completely combined. Let stand until it reaches room temperature. Coat pork on both sides with marinade, but reserve ¾ cup for basting. Cover and refrigerate overnight.

Remove refrigerated porkchops from marinade and sprinkle with salt. Grill chops on medium heat for 15 to 20 minutes, frequently basting with marinade on both sides. Continue to baste as you grill until pork reaches 150-degrees internal temperature. Place a mound of Eseeola's Candied Yams (recipe on next page) in the center of each of 4 warm plates. Prop porkchop up in mixture; drizzle with Eseeola's Apple Cider Pistachio Butter (recipe follows). Serves 4.

Eseeola's Apple Cider Pistachio Butter

1 tablespoon garlic, minced
¼ cup shallots, chopped
2 tablespoons butter
1 cup Calvados or
    Applejack brandy
1 cup cider, freshly pressed
    (if possible)

3 tablespoons cider vinegar
1 cup demi-glace (found in
    specialty shops)
1 chipotle chili, minced
4 tablespoons unsalted butter,
    cut in ½-inch pieces
½ cup pistachios, toasted
    and chopped

In a skillet, sauté garlic and shallots in butter until translucent. Add brandy, cider, and cider vinegar and reduce by half over medium heat. Add demi-glace and reduce until 2 cups of liquid remain. Lower heat and add chipotle. Slowly add butter pieces while whisking constantly. Allow each piece of butter to melt before adding the next until totally emulsified. Pour through China cap strainer into a warm stainless steel container and keep warm. Add chopped nuts. Adjust seasoning. (Sauce will separate if allowed to get too hot.)

Eseeola's Candied Yams, Roasted Apple, and Bananas

1 large sweet potato, peeled
   and diced to ½-inch pieces
1 teaspoon cooking oil
2 Granny Smith apples,
   cored, peeled, and halved
½ cup light brown sugar
¾ cup light rum

½ cup apple cider
3 tablespoons cider vinegar
½ cup unsalted butter, cut in
   ½-inch pieces
2 teaspoons vanilla extract
2 bananas, sliced lengthwise,
   cut in ½-inch pieces

Roast sweet potato on lightly oiled baking pan at 425 degrees until tender and lightly caramelized. In a separate pan, roast apples until tender.

In a sauté pan, caramelize brown sugar over medium heat. Add rum, apple cider, and vinegar and lower heat until sugar has melted, about 5 to 7 minutes. Reduce to glaze consistency. Whisk in butter, piece by piece until incorporated. Whisk in vanilla. Toss sweet potato, apples, and banana in rum butter. Keep warm. Serves 4.

Weaverville Milling
Company

1 Old Mill Lane off Reems Creek Road
WEAVERVILLE

emember Rosie the Riveter, who symbolized women working at traditional male jobs while the men went to fight WW II? Weaverville Milling Company had its own version of Rosie in Margie Duff, who kept the mill wheel grinding the community's flour and meal during the war years. It was an arduous task, but a combination of woman power and willpower kept the operation going.

Weaverville Milling Company is now a restaurant, but remnants of the operation that began in 1912 can still be found on the top floor of the mill. The historic equipment enhances the restaurant's rustic décor.

Dinner
5:00 P.M. TO 9:00 P.M.
daily except Wednesdays
April—December.

Open Thursday—Sunday
in February and March.
Closed in January.

For reservations
call (828) 645-4700.

www.weaverville
milling.com

Guests at the restaurant are free to do more than just have a good meal. Near our table on the main floor was an old jigsaw puzzle, and every now and then a diner would wander over and fit a piece into its place. On the mezzanine, which is decorated with handmade quilts that are for sale, an old-fashioned dollhouse waits for the amusement of children before or after dinner.

Touches of the country are everywhere. Just as we were turning to our seats, a woman placed a lovely bouquet of wild flowers on our table. The colors set off our yellow-and-white checked tablecloth, the yellow pine walls, and the original oak floor.

The menu contained so many of my favorites that I had a hard time making a decision, until I found the Chicken with Raspberry and Rhubarb Sauce. What could be more unusual! The dish was so delicious that I tried to include the recipe here, but neither the chef nor I could figure out a way to break it down to family-size portions.

My daughter Heather chose the very hearty sandwich of Prime Rib Au Jus On Toast with Country Fried Potatoes. On the light side, the Vegetarian Lasagne is a good suggestion, or Fresh Mountain Trout.

Dieters beware: No meal at Weaverville would be complete without the famous desserts. They originate from old local recipes, but each has been given a creative twist under owner Sally A. Smith. The freshest fruit of the season made the Blueberry and Peach Cobbler a standout, especially when topped with Homemade Vanilla Ice Cream.

A taste of Heather's Oatmeal Pie, reminiscent of a pecan pie, made that recipe a must.

I declined the special wine of the day because the homemade apple juice seemed exactly appropriate to this homespun experience. Guests under sixteen or over seventy-five receive a complimentary Slushy, an icy drink of 7-Up and grenadine. This is a terrific treat for all ages and will add a refreshing note to any hot summer day.

Weaverville Milling Company reminds me of an unpolished gem that turns up in a rock collector's pan: a treasure sparkling within a rough exterior.

Weaverville Milling Company's Peach and Blueberry Cobbler

2 cups fresh peaches, sliced
1 cup fresh blueberries
1 teaspoon cinnamon
1 tablespoon lemon juice
1 cup flour
1 teaspoon baking powder
½ teaspoon salt

3 tablespoons margarine, melted
½ cup brown sugar
1 cup white sugar
½ cup milk
1 tablespoon corn starch
1 cup boiling water

Grease a 9-by-9-inch pan and fill with fruit. Sprinkle cinnamon and lemon juice over fruit. Mix flour, baking powder, and salt. Cream margarine, brown sugar and ½ cup white sugar. Sift dry ingredients into creamed mixture, alternately adding milk; mix well. Spread over fruit. Sift ½ cup of white sugar with cornstarch and sprinkle over batter. Pour boiling water over pie. Bake at 350 degrees for about 1 hour. Serves 8 to 10.

Weaverville Milling Company's Slushy

¾ cup 7-Up
1 tablespoon grenadine

¼ cup club soda
6 ice cubes

Place all ingredients in blender and mix until frothy. Serves 1.

Weaverville Milling Company's Oatmeal Pie

1 cup uncooked oats
½ cup margarine, melted
1 teaspoon maple extract
2 tablespoons flour
3 eggs

½ cup white sugar
½ cup brown sugar
1 cup white corn syrup
1 unbaked pie shell

In a medium mixing bowl combine the oats, margarine, maple extract, flour, eggs, sugar, brown sugar, and corn syrup. Mix briskly with a wire whisk until well blended and all tiny lumps are integrated. Pour into the unbaked pie shell. Bake at 350 degrees for 45 to 55 minutes. Yields 1 pie.

Gabrielle's
at Richmond Hill Inn

87 Richmond Hill Drive
3 Miles North of Downtown off U.S. 19/23
ASHEVILLE

$\mathcal{H}$ow does one go about feeding 5,000 for a Fourth of July picnic? The time was 1890, a year after U.S. congressman and ambassador Richmond Pearson and his wife, Gabrielle, built their Victorian mansion. Duty, the congressman believed, required that he invite everyone in Asheville, then about 15,000 people.

Fortunately, Gabrielle had gained experience as a hostess during their foreign posts, and she determined how much fried chicken, potato salad, coconut cake, watermelon, ice tea, and lemonade to have her staff prepare. This successful picnic must have been the reason that the inn's current dining room is named Gabrielle's.

Dinner
6:00 P.M. TO 9:00 P.M.
Wednesdays—Monday
February—December.

Reservations required.
(800) 545-9238
or (828) 252-7313.

www.richmondhillinn.com

There are many ways to set the scene for an elegant dinner, and Gabrielle's employs several of them. You enter through a grand hall paneled in rich native oak. You hear Christopher Leonard's piano tempting you to slow down and dust off the day. In summer, you look out the dining room window and see old-fashioned hollyhocks and larkspurs peeping over the wraparound porch. And the furnishings, though not Pearson originals, were carefully chosen to reflect the way the very rich once lived. For an evening, or longer if you are staying in this romantic inn, you will be pampered, as guests were in Gabrielle's day.

The blonde beauty Gabrielle would have appreciated chef Michelle Kelley's inventiveness with the Ginger Peach-Glazed Gulf Shrimp appetizer. The Chilled Asparagus Soup with Steamed Maine Crab is a recipe that your family will ask for repeatedly, as is Roasted Salmon with Lemon, Herb, and Pine Nut Crust. Equally as wonderful is the tender Lamb with Tart Baked Tomato.

Green Tea Sorbet is a refreshing, healthy palate cleanser, and for dessert a very classy Lavender Crème Brûlée is recommended. Lavender grows quite well in North Carolina.

Gabrielle's Chilled Asparagus Soup with Steamed Maine Crab, and Mint

Soup

4 shallots, peeled and sliced
1 tablespoon oil
2 bunches asparagus, top
⅔ only

about 2 cups heavy cream
1 teaspoon salt

Sweat shallots in oil over medium heat until translucent. Add asparagus, then heavy cream to cover. Add salt. Cook until asparagus is just cooked through, about 8 minutes. Strain cream and reserve. Purée asparagus in food processor, adding reserved cream as necessary. Chill for four hours.

Crab

8 ounces high-quality, fresh
    crab
juice of 1 lemon
¼ teaspoon Dijon mustard

pinches of salt and fresh
    black pepper
2 teaspoons olive oil
8 fresh mint leaves, sliced

Mix ingredients and divide among 4 chilled bowls. In each bowl surround with soup and garnish with fresh sliced mint. Serves 4.

Gabrielle's Green Tea Sorbet

3 cups water
2 green tea bags

1 cup sugar
1¼ cups lemon juice

Boil 2 cups of water and put in 2 green tea bags. Jiggle tea bags and cover to steep. While green tea steeps, put 1 cup of water and sugar in a small saucepan and bring to a boil; lower heat to simmer and cook, stirring, until mixture becomes syrupy. Remove from heat. Remove tea bags after squeezing them into tea to release flavor. Add lemon juice, stir and taste. Add more sugar if needed. Pour mixture into a 9-by-6-by-2-to-3-inch-high metal pan. Cover tightly with 2 layers of aluminum foil and put in freezer until just frozen. Remove and put chunks into food processor and process until sorbet is smooth. Recover, refreeze, and repeat processing if needed. Serves 8 to 12.

Gabrielle's Roasted Salmon with Lemon, Herb, and Pine Nut Crust

Crust

4 tablespoons pine nuts
½ cup parsley, fine-chopped
¼ cup fresh bread crumbs
4 tablespoons butter

1 clove garlic, diced
1 tablespoon lemon juice
segments from half a lemon
½ teaspoon salt

Combine ingredients in a food processor and process until well combined. Remove and place in plastic wrap to form into a 3-by-3-inch block. Chill until firm. Cut into ¼-inch slices. (There may be some left over, which is good to use on vegetables.)

Salmon

4 6-ounce pieces of center-
    cut salmon fillets

salt and pepper to taste
1 tablespoon olive oil

Preheat oven to 425 degrees. Season salmon on both sides with salt and pepper. Heat an oven-safe sauté pan over high-heat with oil until it slides across the pan. Sear the fish until golden brown and cooked a quarter of the way through. Turn fish, and place ½-inch butter slice over each fish. Remove pan to hot oven and cook until butter is melted and slightly brown, about 5 to 7 minutes. Check on fish and don't overcook. Serves 4.

Grove Park Inn
Resort & Spa

290 Macon Avenue
ASHEVILLE

he wind feels cleaner when it sweeps across you on the high balcony of Grove Park Inn.

E.W. Grove, who built the inn in 1913, believed that when the wind blew through the Smoky Mountains' haze it gathered a crispness. For me, that has been true on every visit of the last twenty years. I look forward to the balcony view of the mountains with Asheville snuggled below. Also, a spectacular vista is now available from the elaborate grotto-like spa.

Grove believed that nature could invigorate the weary. With every visit it is awe-inspiring to walk through the interior's granite structure, which was literally hewn out of Sunset Mountain. Grove's philosophy of "thinking big" was part of his desire to create a hotel that would be the epitome of gracious hospitality. The inn's original advertising stated that "All our waiters wear freshly laundered white gloves," and "Guests are encouraged to speak in low tones." The inn was billed not as a sanitarium, but as "a resting place for tired people." I'm always the tired applicant when I arrive.

This time I had dinner at Chops at Sunset Terrace. Twinkling city lights were below, as a dance band played old favorites next door at the Great Bar. My choice was Rainbow Trout, which I knew would be fresh. But this one was different. It was served with a stew comprised of sweet potatoes and smoked trout, in addition to the trout filets. My friend Jane Brock had Duck Breasts that used the old with the new, with tastes that I would not have imagined. We also sampled Prawns in Dijon Sauce with Caramelized Onion. The onion lent an extra zip in that imaginative dish, which I'll order next time. Maybe it was foolish, but we ordered rich desserts and then realized we should have shared the wicked Chocolate Cake, as it was rich enough for two.

All of the Grove Park Inn's five restaurants, except for Pool Cabana at the spa, offer a premium selection of international wines and imported beers. And each restaurant has a different atmosphere. It was originally suggested that "Gentlemen not desiring to dine in evening dress may use the East dining room." You won't find folks in shorts and flip-flops, but after six P.M. men must wear collared shirts

Breakfast
7:30 A.M. to 10:00 A.M.

Lunch
11:30 A.M. to 3:00 P.M.

Dinner
6:00 P.M. to 9:00 P.M.

For reservations call
(800) 438-5800.

www.groveparkinn.com

and long pants. It's important to be able to say that the restaurant's self-imposed requirements for good food are as stringent as they were when I first had lunch here in the former Dogwood Room.

An appetizing way to begin any meal, except breakfast, would be a Sun-dried Tomato Salad accompanied by a Five-Onion Soup. Follow with any of their aged beef dishes. My husband likes their sixteen-ounce Rib Eye with Ravenswood Bordelaise Sauce, which will never go out of style. It will just be gussied up a bit with a new sauce.

After dining, take time to read the inscriptions painted on the stone walls of the lobby. Huge fireplaces at either end are large enough to burn twelve-foot logs. Guests sit in rocking chairs after reading wall quotes of Emerson, Thoreau, and Jefferson. The philosophical inscription that still seems best suited to the era is "Be not simply good, be good for something!"

Grove Park Inn's Sautéed Trout with Sweet Potato Smoked Trout Hash

4 tablespoons butter
½ cup celery, chopped
½ cup red onion, chopped
1 green bell pepper, chopped
1 sweet potato, peeled and cut into ¼-inch cubes, blanched

2 ounces smoked trout, flaked
salt and ground pepper to taste
½ teaspoon fresh sage
½ teaspoon fresh thyme
1 cup and 1 teaspoon flour
8 trout fillets
garnish with lemon slices

Melt 2 tablespoons of butter in a large sauté pan; add celery, onion, and bell pepper. Sauté for 2 minutes or until soft. Add potato and cook 2 minutes or until hot. Add smoked trout, salt, pepper, herbs, and 1 teaspoon of flour. Stir to combine. Dredge trout fillets in remaining flour and place in fillet pan, skin side up. Sauté 3 minutes and turn over gently. Season fillets with salt and fresh ground pepper. Divide prepared hash and place equal amounts in 4 warmed plates. Place 2 trout fillets on each. Garnish with lemon slices. Serves 4.

Grove Park Inn's Duck Breasts

2 tablespoons vegetable oil
4 boneless duck breasts
salt and ground pepper to
    taste
3 shallots, chopped
1 large garlic clove, chopped
    fine

2 tablespoons coffee beans,
    ground with coffee grinder
    or mortar and pestle
2 cups chicken broth
¼ teaspoon dried thyme
2 tablespoons unsalted butter
pinch of brown sugar

Heat oil in a large skillet until hot. Add duck breasts and season with salt and pepper. Sauté, skin side down, for about 4 minutes. Remove from heat (and skillet) and keep warm. Add shallots and garlic to the skillet and sauté for one minute. Combine ground coffee with broth, stirring well. Add mixture to pan, stirring. Add thyme. Lower heat to simmer and cook for 15 minutes, stirring periodically. Strain broth, return liquid to skillet and reduce amount by half. Stir in butter a little at a time to emulsify. Season with salt and pepper and a pinch of brown sugar. Slice duck and top with gravy. Serves 4.

Grove Park Inn's
Fried Swiss Cheese in Beer Batter

3 3-ounce slices Swiss cheese
1 cup flour
1 egg yolk
pinch of salt

2 tablespoons beer
2 egg whites
oil for frying

Bring cheese to room temperature. Mix ½ cup of flour, egg yolk, salt, and beer. Beat egg whites to stiff peaks and fold slowly into batter. Coat cheese slices with flour and dip in batter. Deep fry in vegetable oil. Serve with a salad. Serves 3.

Expressions Restaurant
& Wine Lounge

114 North Main Street
HENDERSONVILLE

*F*or years I've listened to gourmands sing the praises of chef/owner Tom Young's Expressions. Investigating this 1902 downtown Hendersonville building that was constructed of handmade red brick, I looked closely at the exposed brick wall in the classy downstairs dining room; every seventh brick is turned backward. But that is the only backward thing about this award-winning restaurant.

Many chefs who cook as well as Young come to believe that they are the last word in creativity. But Young is so modest that I had to drag out information concerning his awards. Finally a staff member brought me three pages listing his achievements. Shyly he credited the Culinary School at Asheville-Buncombe Technical Community College, listed as third best in the nation, with his success. He tossed off his accolades, saying: "We don't mess with food a lot. It's the flavors you have to work in." Yeah, right.

For an appetizer Young puddled a plate with Hollandaise Sauce, added a Portobello mushroom and topped it with fresh steamed spinach mixed with creamy goat cheese and subtle spices. This combination of flavors delivered a wallop.

Beets, which are often too sweet, were not when Young roasted them. The accompanying sauce was flint-hot with a glimmer of sweet. I was served sweet peas so crunchy-fresh that they must have just been picked. Salmon was roasted to juicy tenderness and was presented with a subtle sauce, allowing the essential flavors to come through.

It can sometimes be difficult to distinguish Young's preparations from those of his protégés, one of whom cooked magic into Hickory Smoked Duck Breast. With this entrée he served Bourbon Sweet Potatoes, topping the side dish with shaved, flash-fried sweet potatoes.

A guest from New York was heard to say, "This is the best lamb I've ever had. I'll salivate every time I think of it."

I sampled two bites of a rich chocolate mousse and thought a li-

Lunch
11:30 A.M. to 2:00 P.M.
Monday—Friday

Sunday Brunch
11:30 A.M. to 2:00 P.M.

Dinner
Begins at 6:00 P.M.
Monday—Saturday

Wine Bar Lounge
5:00 P.M. until

For dinner or brunch reservations, call
(828) 693-8516.

queur had been added. But no, Young ordered this cocoa berry from France. The same dedication to food and wine was evident in the upstairs lounge. The large room with mural walls and comfy leather sofas encouraged conversation.

Before I left, I made Young promise to include me in the classes that he holds from time to time.

Expressions' Bourbon Sweet Potatoes

4 large sweet potatoes
4 tablespoon unsalted butter
¼ cup light brown sugar
3 tablespoons bourbon, or
less

¼ teaspoon vanilla
1 tablespoon cinnamon, or
more to taste
salt and pepper to taste

Preheat oven to 400 degrees. Cook potatoes for about 1 hour, until tender. When cool, peel potatoes, cut flesh into squares and put in an electric mixer. Add remaining ingredients and whip until well combined and without lumps. Taste and adjust seasoning. Serves 8.

Expressions' Roasted Beets with Wilted Beet Greens

12 baby beets
½ teaspoon fresh thyme
leaves
kosher salt and black pepper
to taste

¼ cup olive oil
2 tablespoons balsamic
vinegar

Wash beets thoroughly. Remove greens and trim the ends. Reserve greens. Place the beets in a mixing bowl and toss with thyme leaves, salt, pepper, and half of olive oil (⅛ cup). Place the beets in a shallow baking pan or tray. Cover the pan with foil and roast for about 45 minutes. Remove foil and bake an additional 10 minutes, or until beets are tender. Remove beets from the oven and cool to room temperature. When cooled, the skin will slip off easily by hand. Cut the beets in half. Add remaining olive oil to a sauté pan and heat until smoking; add greens and stir with a spoon. Add balsamic vinegar and stir rapidly. Remove from heat. Adjust seasoning with salt and pepper. Serves 4.

Molasses Glaze

½ cup dark molasses
4 tablespoons Madeira wine
1 tablespoon red wine
  vinegar
1 tablespoon balsamic
  vinegar

2 tablespoons light brown
  sugar
½ teaspoon fresh ginger,
  grated
salt and black pepper to taste

In a stainless steel saucepan over medium heat, add the molasses, Madeira wine, red wine vinegar, balsamic vinegar, brown sugar, and ginger. Stir with a wire whisk until well combined. Continue to stir until ingredients form a light syrupy consistency. Season with salt and pepper. Set aside.

Duck

4 duck breasts or 2 small
  ducks

2 tablespoons olive oil
2 tablespoon hickory dust

Trim away any excess skin and fat. Score skin lightly in a grid pattern, being careful not to cut into the flesh. Season duck on both sides with salt and pepper. Place olive oil in a large sauté pan over medium heat and add the duck. Cook on 1 side only until the skin is brown and crisp. Remove duck from pan. In a stovetop smoker place 2 tablespoons of hickory dust (found at lumber yard) and place duck, skin side up, on the grid pan. Place on stovetop and heat on medium. Smoke for 7 to 8 minutes. Remove duck from smoker and brush with molasses glaze. Let stand 10 minutes before thinly slicing the breast against the grain of the meat. Place Bourbon Sweet Potatoes (recipe on previous page) in a pastry bag and pipe onto a warm dinner plate. Fan out the sliced duck on each plate and drizzle with molasses glaze. Serves 6 or more.

Inn on Church

201 Third Avenue West at Church Street
HENDERSONVILLE

he Inn on Church and its restaurant complement each other well. Out of the fifty historic restaurants that I visited for this book, this was the first. What a great opening act this restaurant is for the fiftieth anniversary of John F. Blair, Publisher, and the twenty-first anniversary of *North Carolina's Historic Restaurants and Their Recipes*.

The list of previous owners of this inn and restaurant, which was built as the Aloha Hotel in 1921, reads like the begats in the Bible. Mrs. Etta Carson lost the inn in 1932 when the Depression caused its auction on the courthouse steps for twenty-five dollars. In 1928 the inn, known as Carson House, was included on the National Register of Historic Properties. The inn has been in continuous use since its origin.

Lunch
11:30 A.M. to 2:00 P.M.
Tuesday—Saturday

Dinner
Begins at 5:00 P.M.
Wednesday—Saturday

For reservations call
(800) 330-3836
or (828) 693-3258.

www.innspiredinns.com

Rhonda and Michael Horton bought the inn in 2000, spending five months on a complete restoration. The Hortons are very inventive, successfully using a bicycle as a flower container and adding other whimsical décor features. They brought in 28-year-old chef Sebastian Carosi and his wife, Melissa Morbillo, a wine steward, who introduced Northern Italian cuisine to the inn.

I sampled almost everything Carosi was preparing in the kitchen and found him to be the king of fusion cooking. He's one of the most exciting young chefs I have encountered, and I have eaten in dining rooms of the world's ten most famous chefs. I never thought I would consider making a three-hour trip to Hendersonville just for dinner, but I would do it again for one of Carosi's meals.

My friend, Jane Brock, and I sat on the inn's side porch. Dinner began with a slice of organic watermelon splashed with tangerine oil, topped with locally produced "farmstead Carolina feta cheese" sprinkled with pepper and edible flower petals. With each bite the combo of sweet melon gently blended with salty feta, then compensated with slight hints of citrusy tangerine. Our second appetizer, Big-Assed Carolina Shrimp with Tuscan White Beans, combined fresh sage and Amish butter, bringing Italy to Carolina in one spoonful. When I told Carosi that I had to have this recipe, he laughed. "You and everyone who eats here. They won't let me take it off the menu."

My entrée was Hickory Nut Smoky Mountain Trout with maple-blended mashed sweet potatoes sitting upon a blackberry and merlot reduction. You can do your own fusion by preparing a bite of nutty trout atop a teaspoon of potatoes snugged with the reduction. I'm telling you, it could replace our traditional turkey Thanksgiving meal.

After dinner, we went out on the wraparound veranda where, being Crème Brûlée freaks, we had Carosi Buttermilk Crème Brûlée. It's another recipe destined to be famous.

Inn on Church's Tuscan White Bean Soup

2 pounds white beans, dried
4 cups water
6-8 baby carrots, sliced
2 stalks celery, chopped
1 medium red onion, chopped
1 smoked ham hock
2 bay leaves

1 teaspoon thyme
1-2 sprigs rosemary, stripped
1 teaspoon sage
sea salt and pepper to taste
½ cup Parmigiano-Reggiano rind

Put rinsed beans in water in a large pot and let soak overnight. Empty and fill with 1 1/2 quarts new water; bring to a boil. Lower heat to simmer and add beans, carrots, celery, onion, ham hock, bay leaves, thyme, rosemary, and sage. Stir to combine and let cook for about an hour. Stir in salt and pepper and let cook for 15 minutes. Remove ham hock and ladle soup into 8 to 10 bowls. Chop rind fine and sprinkle over each bowl. Serves 8 to 10.

Inn on Church's Chicken, Apple, and Spiced Pecan Salad

3 cups "free range" chicken, boiled
1 rib of organic celery, diced
¼ Vidalia onion, diced
½ Granny Smith apple, diced
¼ cup spiced pecans
½-1 cup mayonnaise

2 tablespoons stone-ground mustard
2 tablespoons wildflower honey
½ teaspoon prepared horseradish
2 dashes Tabasco sauce
2 dashes Worcestershire sauce
½ teaspoon kosher salt
pinch of fresh ground pepper

Keep chicken in boiling liquid until it reaches room temperature. Remove and tear into bite-size pieces. Put chicken and all vegetables and fruits into a large bowl and stir well. Add mayonnaise and stir until completely incorporated. Add remaining ingredients; stir until flavors have blended. Taste and adjust seasoning. Cover and refrigerate for at least 2 hours. Serves 8 to 12.

Inn on Church's Lemonade Vinaigrette

2 tablespoons hot water
2 tablespoons sugar
3 tablespoons rice wine
   vinegar
½ cup lemon juice
½ teaspoon cracked pepper

¾ teaspoon kosher salt
1 teaspoon wildflower honey
1 teaspoon fresh thyme leaves
⅓ cup fresh mint, chopped
½ teaspoon lemon zest
3 tablespoons grape seed oil

In a stainless steel bowl mix water with sugar with a whisk until it dissolves. Add all remaining ingredients and mix well. Mix again before dressing salad. Cover and refrigerate for later use. Yields about 1 cup.

Saluda Grade Café

Main Street

SALUDA

When a drugstore soda shop was built on Main Street in 1945, the help was paid a whopping twenty-five cents an hour. That has changed, but little else has in Saluda, home of the nation's steepest railroad grade. The Saluda Grade Café's name pays tribute to that engineering distinction. A storefront window featuring an antique porcelain woodstove, stenciled with red roses, welcomes visitors to the Saluda Grade Café. The whole town looks like a set for a 1940s movie, and the citizens seem to be as friendly and helpful as in that often idealized era.

Lunch
11:00 A.M. to 3:00 P.M.
Tuesday — Sunday

Dinner
5:00 P.M. to 9:00 P.M.
Wednesday — Saturday

For reservations call
(828) 749-5854.

Co-owner Carol Thompson was arranging sweet-smelling pink roses when my friend Jane Brock and I walked in. The proprietor of the Purple Onion Restaurant (a few doors down) had given the roses to Thompson for an evening party. "Isn't she your competition?" I asked. "Oh, no," Thompson said, "We don't have competition here. Everyone helps everyone else."

Today this historic red brick, two-story building is one of Saluda's favorite hangouts. Folks come from all around to catch up on what's happening, to check out original paintings by community and regional artists, or to buy one of the mosaic planters made by Lake Lure's Ben Weidel. (Also for sale are Bill Dippel's picture frames, made from wine corks. Proceeds go to Saluda's Senior Center.) But most people come here for the excellent food. As one patron said, "It's just plain good, and most of it is good for you, too!" Those accolades are what owners Kaye Strang and Carol Thompson have strived for since opening the café in 1998.

We dropped by for a late lunch, which began with fresh Tomato Basil Soup. This soup, thankfully, never encountered the canned variety. The freshness truly is identifiable from the first spoonful. A scrumptious, fresh Chicken and Grape Salad followed. The plate included wholesomely arranged fresh pineapple, strawberries, and cantaloupe. I tasted Jane's Black & Blue Salad, made with blue cheese and spicy blackened chicken. I'll order it next time.

Be sure to order the homemade Carolina Pie. This chocolate, coconut, and pecan dessert will remind you of your favorite candy bar from childhood. It's a winner, just like this homey little café that also serves dinner.

Saluda Grade Café's Tomato Basil Soup

6 cups fresh or canned diced
   tomatoes
6 cups water
½ cup chopped onion
1 bay leaf

1 tablespoon fresh chopped
   garlic
½ cup fresh leaf basil,
   chopped
2 cups heavy cream

Place all ingredients except cream in a stockpot and cook on high until vegetables are done. Remove from heat. Use a blender to purée soup until smooth. Temper in two cups of heavy cream. Cover and refrigerate. Serves 10 to 12.

Saluda Grade Café's Carolina Pie

½ cup butter, unsalted
1 cup granulated sugar
3 large eggs
1 cup chocolate chips
½ cup coconut

½ cup pecans, chopped
1 teaspoon pure vanilla
   extract
½ teaspoon bourbon
1 prepared 9-inch pie shell

Preheat oven to 350 degrees. Cream butter and sugar with an electric mixer until smooth. Add eggs, one at a time. Mix until smooth. Add chocolate chips, coconut, and pecans. Stir in vanilla extract and bourbon. Pour into pie shell and bake for 45 to 50 minutes, or until pie is set. Serves 6.

Saluda Grade Café's Chicken and Grape Salad

1 pound white meat chicken
1 cup celery, chopped
1 cup seedless red grapes, cut
  in half

1 cup mayonnaise
1 tablespoon fresh lemon juice
1 teaspoon thyme
salt and pepper to taste

In a large bowl mix all ingredients thoroughly, cover and chill.
Serves 10 to 12.

The Greystone Inn

Greystone Lane

LAKE TOXAWAY

I awoke at Greystone Inn, opened my window, and saw Lake Toxaway shimmering through the morning's mist. In 1914 the wealthy Lucy Armstrong fell in love with this same spot, and this arbiter of fine taste begged her husband, George, to build a summer home beside the lake. He agreed, with one stipulation: She must "rough it" for a summer on the spot of their intended home. Lucy complied by having a 2,000-square-foot tent erected, with ten servants to manage it.

In 1915 the Armstrongs moved into their newly built nineteen-bedroom summer home; Mr. Armstrong died in 1924. Lucy and her daughter, also named Lucy, continued to entertain guests at Greystone for weeks on end with lavish dinner parties. "Miss Lucy's" sense of style and innovative cuisine became legendary.

Tim Lovelace and Reg Heinitsh, Jr., bought Miss Lucy's summer home a mere three days before it was scheduled for demolition. Greystone Inn is now on the National Register of Historic Places, and is one of the most comprehensive renovations that I've seen. Elegance and superb food combine in an atmosphere where guests are reminded of a gentler time. The staff makes you feel like you are one of Miss Lucy's privileged set. It's the little things: gourmet meals, a spa, golf course, tea on the sun porch, an afternoon champagne cruise around Lake Toxaway, cocktails in the library. After you've been on the road, it is nirvana. Guests and those just stopping for a meal admit that chef Chris McDonald's famed cuisine is as good as friends proclaim.

After two visits I can say that the food prepared by McDonald, who has been at the inn for fifteen years, is worth the trip. The restaurant is located in the original boathouse and the view of the lake is superb. I began with an inspired Corn and Lobster Chowder, with a flavor rich and round. I could have made a whole meal with the addition of light and flaky biscuits, but I knew that quail was ahead.

When you see a talented presentation, you know the chef cares. My quail looked like a bird's nest surrounded by vegetables, and it was fun to untangle. Quail is usually much better than chicken, and when cooked with mushrooms, fois gras, and brandy it is one full-strength taste. The vegetables were the perfect complement.

That evening the palate cleanser was minted apple sorbet, which set me up for Deep Dish Buttermilk Pie. It is surprising how different buttermilk pies can taste, with this one reminding me of a cheesecake.

On each visit I've met honeymooners or anniversary celebrants at the afternoon tea or the cocktail hour. Could you imagine a more romantic or secluded place?

Greystone Inn's Boneless Quail "Soufflé" in Crust

2 cups Shiitake
  mushrooms
2 cups button mushrooms
1 tablespoon clarified butter
6 ounces foie gras

salt and pepper to taste
2 tablespoons brandy
2 boneless quail
6 egg whites
puff pastry

Coarse chop the mushrooms and sauté them in a medium-size sauté pan in butter. Add fois gras (found in specialty shops and some grocers) and sauté. Sprinkle with salt and pepper and mix in 1 tablespoon of brandy. Purée mushroom mixture in a food processor, remove, wrap, and chill for 2 hours. Lay quail on a cutting board and season with salt, pepper, and remaining brandy. Put the mixed mushrooms in the center of the quail, and brush it with the egg wash. Place sufficient amount of puff pastry to wrap the quail on the cutting board. After wrapping, pinch pastry ends together and brush the whole wrapping with egg wash. Bake at 375 degrees for 20 minutes. Serves 2.

Vegetables

2 potatoes, peeled and
  matchstick cut
2 or more cups of vegetable oil
2 carrots, peeled, cut with
  melon baller

2 zucchini, peeled, cut with
  melon baller
2 turnips, peeled, cut with
  melon baller
2-3 cups chicken broth or stock
2 or more tablespoons butter

Deep fry potatoes in a sufficient amount of oil until done. Poach carrots, zucchini, and turnips in chicken broth and finish with butter. Remove and purée in food processor. Surround the quail with the potatoes and place the remaining vegetables around the potatoes. Serves 2 to 3.

Graham Cracker Crust

2 cups crumbled graham
  crackers

½ cup butter or more
⅓ cup sugar

Combine all ingredients and mix by hand. Pat evenly into a 10-inch springform pan, working crust onto sides. Set aside.

1 pound cream cheese
3 cups sugar
1 cup sour cream
8 large eggs

½ cup heavy cream
2 cups buttermilk
1 tablespoon vanilla

Let cream cheese soften for an hour and cut into 1-inch squares. In an electric mixer combine the cream cheese, sugar, and sour cream. Add one egg at a time and mix until blended. Add heavy cream and buttermilk, mixing well. Add vanilla and stir. Slowly pour mixture into graham-cracker-crust pan. Bake in a 350 degree oven for 1 hour and 15 minutes, or until pie is set. (When it starts to crack on top, the pie is done.) Remove from oven, cover and chill. Serves 16.

Brown Sugar Sauce

1 pound light brown
  sugar

1 quart heavy cream
2 cups sour cream

In a saucepan add all ingredients and mix. Cook on medium heat until mixture reduces to ⅓. Pour in container with a lid and chill until served over pie.

High Hampton Inn

1525 N.C. 107 South

CASHIERS

After sitting in a rocker on the back porch balcony at High Hampton Inn, you begin to feel serene. Maybe that's why second and third generations of folks, who were brought here as youngsters, come back. No one gets tired of the view of Hampton Lake that curls at the base of Rock and Chimney Top mountains. It's a spectacle and spectacles always make me hungry.

I went down to the luncheon buffet line and right away noticed that the dining room had been prettied-up since my last visit. The food is arranged more attractively and the room, which is still homespun, wears a sunnier look. I helped myself to shrimp, fruit salads, Spanish Eggplant, roasted potatoes, fresh melon, and two desserts. It was lucky that they were serving Black Bottom Pie, which is a rich delight. I also squeezed in a few bites of Blueberry Cobbler. The inn still has a variety of broiled fish that is sauced in several ways, as well as dishes you might find at a church picnic. Even though I always have iced tea, I like the idea of serving lemonade, too.

Open daily mid-April to mid-November, and Wednesday to Sunday Thanksgiving week.

Breakfast
7:00 A.M. to 9:30 A.M.

Lunch
12:15 P.M. to 2:15 P.M.

Dinner
6:30 P.M. to 8:15 P.M.

Rock Mountain Tavern
6:00 P.M. to 10:00 P.M.

For reservations call
(828) 743-2411 or
fax (800) 334-2551.

www.highhamptoninn.com

E.L. McKee, the grandfather of the present owner, built the present structure at High Hampton in 1922. However, socializing at the inn dates back to 1791 when Wade Hampton, the Confederate general as well as governor of South Carolina, built his retreat in the Cashiers Valley. He was not the only prominent figure to own the property; his daughter, Caroline, married Dr. William Stewart Halsted, who was head of Johns Hopkins Hospital and is credited with inventing rubber surgical gloves, localized anesthesia, and a surgical technique that is still practiced in some hospitals. Caroline much preferred the unpretentious life of supervising the landscaping of her dahlia garden at High Hampton to the society life in Baltimore. I was pleased that her garden had a number of additions since my last visit and continues to be another lovely place for a walk around the well-kept grounds.

High Hampton Inn's Black Bottom Pie

Crust

1½ cups crushed Zwieback
   crackers
¼ cup powdered sugar

6 tablespoons melted butter
1 teaspoon cinnamon

Mix all ingredients well and pat out evenly into a deep 9-inch pie pan. Bake at 300 degrees for 15 minutes. Cool.

Chocolate Filling

1 tablespoon gelatin
¼ cup cold water
2 cups half-and-half
4 egg yolks (reserve 3 whites)

1 cup sugar
4 teaspoons cornstarch
½ teaspoon vanilla
¼ cup chocolate, melted

Soak gelatin in cold water. Scald half-and-half. Beat egg yolks, and add sugar and cornstarch. Place in double boiler and stir half-and-half in gradually; keep stirring until custard coats a spoon, about 20 minutes. Remove from heat and pour out 1 cup of custard. Add chocolate to cup of custard and beat until well blended and cool. Add vanilla to mixture and pour into pie shell. Add gelatin to remaining custard; cool, but do not allow to stiffen.

To Complete Custard Filling

3 egg whites
¼ teaspoon salt
¼ teaspoon cream of tartar

¼ cup sugar
1 teaspoon almond extract

Make stiff meringue by beating egg whites with salt until frothy. Add cream of tartar and beat until stiff enough to hold a peak, then gradually beat in sugar until very stiff. While remaining custard is still soft, fold in meringue very gently, blend in almond extract, and chill. Pour over chocolate custard.

Topping

1 cup heavy whipping cream   2 tablespoons powdered sugar

Whip the cream, add powdered sugar, and spread over top of pie. Chill until served. Yields 1 pie.

High Hampton Inn's Spanish Eggplant

1 large eggplant
1 teaspoon salt
4 tablespoons butter
½ cup chopped onions
½ cup chopped green pepper
1 14½-ounce can tomatoes
¼ cup brown sugar

4 tablespoons Parmesan
  cheese
1 teaspoon salt, or to taste
½ teaspoon or more white
  pepper
½ teaspoon garlic powder
½ cup bread crumbs

In a saucepan dissolve 1 teaspoon salt in a pint of water. Peel and cube eggplant and parboil in salted water. In separate skillet melt 2 tablespoons butter and sauté onions and green pepper; set aside. Drain eggplant and tomatoes and mix together in a greased casserole. Season with brown sugar, 2 tablespoons Parmesan cheese, salt, white pepper, and garlic powder. Add onions and green pepper and mix thoroughly. Melt remaining butter and drizzle over bread crumbs. Sprinkle crumbs and remaining cheese over vegetables. Bake at 350 degrees for 35 to 40 minutes or until brown. Serves 4.

The Log Cabin

130 Log Cabin Lane
HIGHLANDS

*L*ife in the quaint mountain town of Highlands has changed considerably since Joe Webb built one of his log cabins as a summer home in 1924. When the cabin was converted to a restaurant, its historically sensitive renovators insisted on retaining the original chinking, a ceiling that had never needed repair, and outlets placed five feet up from the floor. Highlands is proud of its jewels-in-the-rough, and one week before my visit the town sponsored a tour of Webb's log homes.

Folks from all over the country visit The Log Cabin because they've heard about its famous coconut cake and excellent steaks. Owners Phil and Sandy Coppage had not even worked in a restaurant before opening The Log Cabin, but they became successful because they hired great chefs.

Open daily
June — November.

December — May open
Wednesday — Sunday.

Dinner
Begins at 5:30 P.M.

For reservations call
(828) 526-3380
or fax (828) 526-1825.

Today, Sandy's coconut cake is so famous that some customers check to make sure it's on the menu before making reservations. This is a cake that has been known to jiggle memory. One afternoon a woman rushed in begging for a piece of the cake. She was told that the restaurant wasn't open, but the excited woman explained that her husband had suffered a stroke and had not been able to talk until they passed The Log Cabin Restaurant. She said, "He looked up and said, 'Coconut cake!'" The no longer silent man got his piece of coconut cake, and a spare for emergencies.

Had it been winter, I would have been beside the fireplace, but on a nice summer night the patio was ideal. The steak was as juicy and tender as promised, and I was told that the key to cooking a good steak rests in the cut of meat, which you'll find in Kansas Beef's, Sterling Silver.

As I ate Pistachio Salmon I learned that the trick was dipping it in coatings, with pistachios coming last. This was similar to one in an earlier edition that I did with chicken and pecans. This fast and easy salmon tastes like you took forever.

Since the Coppages and I all come from Texas, it would have been a sin not to sample the Quail & Cabin-Style Grits. If you like Shrimp and Grits, you're going to like the dish with quail, which Texans claim is better than chicken. Mine was very tender and without a gamey taste.

After all the coconut cake stories, my taste buds were primed for a slice. Unfortunately, the last piece had gone when I arrived. In truth, it was hard to imagine how it could taste better than Banana Walnut Crunch Bread Pudding, which is a lot like Bananas Foster. But I did get their coconut cake recipe.

Log Cabin's Coconut Cake

2 boxes butter cake mix
1 15-ounce can cream of coconut
juice drained from 1 8¼ ounce can of pineapple
1 jigger of rum (optional)
2 cans of crushed pineapple, drained

2 8-ounce bars of cream cheese
1 box of confectioners' sugar
1 cup toasted pecans, fine-chopped
1½ quarts heavy whipping cream
5-6 tablespoons confectioners' sugar

Prepare cakes according to package directions and pour into 4 greased 8- or 9-inch pans. Bake, then cool on wire racks. Combine cream of coconut, pineapple juice from 1 can, and rum. Turn out cakes and spread both sides liberally with coconut cream mixture. For filling, mix crushed pineapple, cream cheese, sugar, and nuts. Spread between cake layers and on top. To ice cake, whip cream in a cold bowl with cold beaters. Gradually add sugar to the cream until cream forms stiff peaks. Spread icing on cake and refrigerate. Serves 12 to 16.

Log Cabin's Pistachio Salmon with Citrus Crust

1 cup flour
1½ cups buttermilk
1½ cups pistachio nuts,
*   shelled and chopped*
4 6-ounce fillets of salmon

2 tablespoons vegetable oil
¼ cup lime juice
¼ cup lemon juice
1 cup orange juice
1 cup sugar

Put 3 flat bowls on cutting board. Fill one with flour, the next with buttermilk and the last with nuts. Dip each fillet of salmon in flour, then buttermilk, then nuts and place on large flat dish. Heat a large (cast-iron if possible) skillet with vegetable oil on medium until hot. Carefully place each fillet in the skillet and cook for 2 to 3 minutes on both sides, depending on thickness. (Do not overcook.) Put salmon in oven at 350 degrees for 20 minutes. While baking, mix juices and sugar in a medium-size pot on medium-high heat. Lower heat and simmer about 15 minutes until mixture is reduced to half. Remove salmon from the oven. Place each fillet on a warm plate and top with sauce. Serves 4.

Log Cabin's Bourbon Sweet Potatoes

8-10 medium to large sweet
*   potatoes*
1 cup brown sugar
½ cup pure maple syrup

½ cup butter, melted
1 teaspoon vanilla
pinch of salt
bourbon to taste

Boil potatoes until tender. Cool until ready for peeling. Place in a large, deep pan and whip with an electric mixer. Add sugar, syrup, and butter, mixing until combined. Add vanilla and salt and 2 tablespoons of bourbon. Mix until smooth and taste. Add extra sugar and bourbon if desired. Serves 10 to 12.

Fryemont Inn

245 Fryemont Inn Road
BRYSON CITY

o you like rustic places where you can sit in a sturdy old rocker on the porch and watch mountain ridges do a color fade from darkest blue to pale periwinkle? That's where I had coffee and a slice of Fryemont Inn Restaurant's Buttermilk Pie. Dessert followed a good dinner in a spacious dining room that's been serving "home-cooked" food since the bark-sided inn was built in 1923.

Afternoons in the mountains can, occasionally, get hot, and the day was perfect for a swim in the secluded swimming pool. When I walked into the inn's great room it was like stepping into a *Saturday Evening Post* cover. Adults and children were playing checkers, reading books, and knitting by the room's massive, unlit stone fireplace.

It didn't take long to get acquainted and discover that the Fryemont has a ghost named Eugenia, who was the niece of Amos Frye. Apparently Eugenia was a sad young artist, whom the inn's housekeeper often found weeping inconsolably. The second floor hallway, which a guest described as looking like it came out of the film *The Shining*, is where you'll see Eugenia's paintings. And according to the staff and repeat residents, Eugenia is still about. Her favorite books fall to the floor and doors slam with unexplained force. No one takes much notice as they realize that Eugenia is in one of her sad periods.

I decided to order the Eugenia Fried Trout coated in cornflour. The trout, caught not far from the inn, was especially good served with mushroom stuffing, which guests call "mushroom business." This recipe could become another reliable comfort dish for me. A host of good fresh vegetables were served with meals, and Zucchini with Cheese was a standout. I also enjoyed glazed baby carrots and good red potatoes.

For dessert I was split between Bread Pudding with Amarreto Sauce and Buttermilk Pie. I chose the pie, which reminded me of a rich chess.

A mountain hideaway lets you sit and rock while you savor each bite, knowing that you don't have to wash dishes, or even make up your bed.

Fryemont Inn's Broccoli Cheddar Bake

1 head fresh broccoli florets,
    or 2 boxes frozen broccoli
2 egg yolks, beaten slightly
½ cup sour cream
1 tablespoon flour
¼ teaspoon salt
dash of pepper
½ teaspoon dry mustard

2 tablespoons onion, chopped
    fine
2 egg whites, beaten stiffly
3 tablespoons butter
1 cup mushrooms, sliced
½ cup shredded Cheddar cheese
½ cup bread crumbs

Steam broccoli until barely tender and drain well. Combine egg yolks with sour cream, flour, salt, pepper, mustard, and onions. Fold in egg whites. Butter a casserole dish with a tablespoon of butter. Layer half the broccoli and egg mixture and half of mushrooms and cheese; repeat. Combine remaining butter and breadcrumbs and sprinkle over the surface. Bake in a preheated 325 degree oven for 30 minutes or until done. Serves 4.

Fryemont Inn's Buttermilk Pie

4 eggs
¼ cup sugar
½ cup buttermilk
¼ cup butter (melted and
    cooled)

1 teaspoon vanilla
1 teaspoon butter flavor
1 unbaked pie crust

Beat eggs and sugar in a medium bowl until fluffy. Add buttermilk and melted butter; stir until just mixed. Stir in vanilla and butter flavor. Pour mixture into a piecrust and bake in a preheated 375-degree oven for 45 minutes or until center is almost set, but still soft. Cool to room temperature and refrigerate. Yields 1 pie.

Fryemont Inn's Mushroom Business

2 cups fresh mushrooms,
    sliced
3 tablespoons butter
½ cup onion, chopped
½ cup green pepper, chopped
½ cup celery, chopped
¼ teaspoon salt
dash of pepper

¼ cup mayonnaise
6 slices whole grain bread
2 eggs, beaten
1 cup milk
1 can cream of mushroom
    soup, undiluted
1 cup shredded Monterey Jack
    or Swiss cheese

Sauté the mushrooms in 2 tablespoons of butter for 3 minutes. Combine onion, green pepper, celery, salt, pepper, mayonnaise, and sautéed mushrooms in a bowl and mix well.

Grease an 8-inch square casserole dish with remaining butter. Cut each bread slice into quarters. Lay half the pieces in the bottom of the casserole dish, overlapping slightly. Spread the mushroom mixture evenly over the bread. Top with remaining bread squares.

In a small bowl, combine eggs and milk. Pour over the bread slices. Cover and refrigerate for 4 hours or overnight. Spread soup over mixture and bake in a 350-degree oven for 45 minutes. Sprinkle with cheese and bake an additional 10 minutes. Serves 6.

Jarrett House

U.S. 23 Business at U.S. 441 South

DILLSBORO

$\mathcal{I}$wenty years ago when I came to Jarrett House, the first words I overheard when entering the dining room were, "I could make a whole meal out of these biscuits alone." That phrase has no doubt been said many times since. Though the restaurant is still owned by Jim and Jean Hartbarger, the second generation is now in charge. Sharon, the Hartbargers' daughter-in-law, assured me that their country-style cuisine is as popular today as it was on my first visit. Once again I sampled a biscuit, then Fried Catfish prepared as it was when I was growing up.

Since vegetables are a favorite I looked forward to fresh green beans, as well as specially prepared beets. Jarrett House serves Squash Casserole using a recipe that has brought many raves throughout the years.

Breakfast
7:00 A.M to 9:00 A.M
Saturday and Sunday.

Lunch
11:30 A.M to 2:30 P.M.

Dinner
4:00 P.M. to 8:00 P.M.
daily, April through October.

For reservations call
(800) 972-5623
or (828) 586-0265.

www.jarretthouse.com

My waiter told me that their Country Ham is almost as good as his grandma's. I've never been a Country Ham fan, but thought I should try a little and did not find it overly salted or hard to chew. I also sampled a bit of their terrific Rainbow Trout, which comes fresh from a neighborhood hatchery. That duo plus "all you can stuff" Fried Chicken are the entrées that have made Jarrett House famous.

Throughout the years I have prepared the restaurant's Vinegar Pie for customers to sample at trade shows and autograph events because it is quick, easy, and inexpensive. I never tell people the pie's name until after they have tasted it. The word vinegar is a bit off-putting, and it's fun to read the shock on faces when I explain. Some say it tastes like lemon and others say pecan, but no one has ever guessed vinegar.

The 1884 house will bring back childhood memories of stuffing yourself at Grandma's. It was "prettied up" a bit by Jim and Jean Hartbarger, and even more so by Sharon and Jim, Jr. They have been careful not to disturb its quaint atmosphere or the Victorian-style parlor.

This three-story rambling white structure, built by the man for whom Dillsboro was named, is encircled with wrought-iron porches. The turn-of-the-century traveler could get a bed and feed for his horse for a quarter. Meals were a dime extra. Later the inn was sold to Robert Frank Jarrett, who cured hams upstairs. In the basement near the natural sulphur spring a concoction was produced that neighbors said smelled peculiarly like alcohol.

That was not the only scandal to come out of the house. During the roar of the twenties two young ladies from Edenton are reported to have shocked half the town when they lit up cigarettes right on the front porch. Today brown bagging is permitted, and some partake of refreshment in the upstairs lounge. Few seem to feel comfortable bringing their brown bags downstairs to the dining room, however.

People of all types enjoy the food. And if you have the time you can sleep in one of the lovely bedrooms upstairs, furnished with antiques and lacking intrusive telephones and televisions. When staying here you relax, with the mountains nestled right behind the inn's back door.

Jarrett House's Pickled Beets

1 onion, medium-size
1 15-ounce can beets

½ cup vinegar
1 cup sugar

Slice onion thin. Mix in a bowl with beets, juice, vinegar, and sugar. Cover and refrigerate for several hours or overnight. Serves 4 to 6.

Jarrett House's Squash Casserole

*1 pound squash, fresh or
    canned, sliced*
1 medium onion, chopped
*6 slices bacon, cooked and
    crumbled*

*5 to 6 leftover biscuits or
    cornbread, crumbled fine*
salt and pepper to taste
*3 to 4 tablespoons melted
    butter*

Cook squash until almost tender. Drain and place in greased, flat, ovenproof pan. Add onions, bacon, and crumbled biscuits on top. Pour melted butter over biscuits. Bake at 350 for 30 minutes, or until golden brown. Serves 4.

Jarrett House's Vinegar Pie

½ cup margarine, melted
2 tablespoons flour
2 tablespoons vinegar
3 eggs

1½ cups sugar
1 tablespoon vanilla extract
1 9-inch pie shell, unbaked

Combine first six ingredients, blending well. Pour into pie shell. Bake at 300 degrees for 45 minutes, or until filling begins to firm. Yields 1 pie.

Index

Chocolate Chess Pie, Angus Barn, 55
Coconut Pie, Colonial Inn, 51
Deep Dish Buttermilk Pie, Greystone Inn, 184
Lemon Meringue Pie, Henry F. Shaffner House, 112
Oatmeal Pie, Weaverville Milling Company, 160
Pecan Pie with Bourbon Crème, Beaufort Grocery, 20
Vinegar Pie, Jarrett House, 200

Puddings, Soufflés, Tarts, Etc.:
Almond Bread Pudding, Undercurrent Restaurant, 104
Apple Tart, Crippen's Restaurant, 144
Banana Cream Pudding, Sam & Omie's, 11
Chocolate-Kahlúa Espresso Truffles, River House, 131
Godiva Chocolate Soufflé with Chocolate Grand Marnier Sauce, Owens' Restaurant, 8
Grand Marnier Marinated Berries with Champagne Sabayon, Undercurrent Restaurant, 103-4
Jenny Fitch's Chocolate Soufflé, Fearrington House, 83-84
Peach and Blueberry Cobbler, Weaverville Milling Company, 159
Peaches and Cream, Ellerbe Springs Inn, 96
Pistachio Tuille Batter, Circa 1922, 40
Raspberry Grand Marnier Parfait, Angus Barn, 55
Strawberry Cobbler, Shatley Springs Inn, 136
Sweet Potato Bread Pudding, Carolina CrossRoads, 80
Sweet Potato Crème Brûlée, Carolina CrossRoads, 80

White Chocolate Mousse with Whipped Cream, McNinch House, 124

Sorbets:
Blueberry Sorbetto, Pop's Trattoria, 71
Green Tea Sorbet, Gabrielle's at Richmond Hill, 163

Dressings, Sauces, Vinaigrettes
Apple Cider Pistachio Butter, Eseeola Lodge, 155-56
Arugula Pesto Sauce, Second Empire, 64
Balsamic Vinaigrette, Anotherthyme, 68
Balsamic Vinaigrette, Luigi's Restaurant, 48
Brown Sugar Sauce, Greystone Inn, 184
Buerre Rouge Sauce, Holly Inn, 88
Capers and Red Pepper Emulsion Sauce, Second Empire, 63
Capers Butter Sauce, Lifesaving Station at The Sanderling, 4
Cornish Game Hen's Braising Liquid, River House, 132
Curry Oil, Liberty Oak Restaurant, 99
Fajita Marinade, Las Palmas, 119
Fig and Sun-Dried Tomato Dressing, Morel's, 151
Granny Smith Dressing, Southern Roots, 107
Greek Marinade, Anotherthyme, 67
Horseradish Sauce, Mast Farm Inn, 147
Lemon Chambertin Buerre Blanc, Holly Inn, 88
Lemon Vinaigrette, Circa 1922, 39
Lemonade Vinaigrette, Inn on Church, 176

Mango Chutney, Pewter Rose, 128

Pico de Gallo, Las Palmas, 120

Salad Nouveau Dressing, Harvey's Mansion, 27

Sherry Vinaigrette, The Cottage, 44

Tomato-Vodka Sauce, McNinch House, 124

Entrées

Fowl:

Blue Cheese Chicken, Southern Roots, 108

Boneless Quail "Soufflé" in Crust, Greystone Inn, 183

Chicken Marsala, Caffe Phoenix, 35

Chicken with Fajitas, Las Palmas, 119

Cornish Game Hens, River House, 132

Duck Breasts, Grove Park Inn, 168

Greek Chicken, Anotherthyme, 67

Hickory-Smoked Duck Breast with Molasses Glaze, Expressions Restaurant, 172

Indonesian Chicken, Pewter Rose, 127

Lemon Chicken, Luigi's Restaurant, 47

Moravian Chicken Pie, Old Salem Tavern, 115

Rosemary Fire-Roasted Chicken, The Cottage, 43

Meats:

Balsamic and Tupelo Honey-Glazed Porkchops, Tupelo's Restaurant, 76

Chili-Glazed Porkchop with Apple Cider Pistachio Butter, Eseeola Lodge, 155-56

Filet Mignon, Circa 1922, 39

Filet Mignon with Gorgonzola Pancetta Butter, Henry F. Shaffner House, 111

Meat Loaf, Ellerbe Springs Inn, 95

Michelina's Meatballs, Luigi's Restaurant, 47

Sweet and Spicy Lamb Marinade, Pewter Rose, 128

Miscellaneous:

Apple Cider Pistachio Butter, Eseeola Lodge, 204

Burgundy Butter, Holly Inn, 87

Gorgonzola Pancetta Butter, Henry F. Shaffner House, 111

Saganaki, Beaufort Grocery, 20

Spanish Omelet, Yana's, 31

Spinachi, Caffe Phoenix, 36

Seafood:

Artichoke Shrimp, Colonial Inn, 51

Big Bowl of Mussels, Pop's Trattoria, 71

Columbia River King Salmon, Second Empire, 63

Curried Scallops, Liberty Oak Restaurant, 99

Dover Sole Paupiettes, Holly Inn, 88

Flounder Stuffed with Jumbo Lump Crabmeat, Lifesaving Station at The Sanderling, 4

Honey- and Tamari-Seared Salmon, Morel's, 151-52

Horseradish-Crusted Salmon, Crippen's Restaurant, 143

Linguine with White Clam Sauce, Sam & Omie's, 11

Lobster Tail with Tomato-Vodka Sauce, McNinch House, 124

Miss O's Crab Cakes, Owens' Restaurant, 8

Pistachio Salmon with Citrus Crust, Log Cabin, 192

Roasted Salmon, Gabrielle's at Richmond Hill Inn, 164

Sautéed Crab Cakes, Second Empire, 64